D0945873

HARRY A. WILMER

HOW DREAMS HELP

How Dreams Help

Written and Illustrated by

Harry A. Wilmer

DAIMON

Cover picture: "Excalibur," a yarn picture made by Harry Wilmer, based on an image from a dream, as described by his journal entry of August 7, 1988:

"The white aura around the sword which is in The Tree of Life has a golden arm on each side. The sword in the tree denotes the sharp edge of discrimination, the power of the rational mind. The blood-red roots of the tree are deep feelings connecting with the unconscious. Black appears around the tree trunk reminding me of the shadow's omnipresence. The tree flourishes, as indicated by the bird-like leaves. Power is indicated by the bolts of red energy from consciousness striking into the earth with sun energy reflected from the arms of the cross. Outside the green boundary of the pure white light is a cross arm, yellow intuition, reaching up into the stylized aura of the sky, while the deep green border of the white is repeated as the boundary demarking the limit of the intrusions into mother earth."

Deep appreciation to the Catto Charitable Trust of San Antonio, Texas, for a grant to help support publication of this book

Photo of the author by Marsha Miller

ISBN 3-85630-582-3

Printed in Canada

To Jane

In times when passions are beginning to take charge of the conduct of human affairs, one should pay less attention to what men of experience and common sense are thinking than to what is preoccupying the imagination of dreamers.

– Alexis de Tocqueville
Democracy in America

CONTENTS

Part IV Control of The Mind

Part V Good

Appendix

Now the study of dreams presents a special difficulty: the fact that we cannot examine dreams directly. We can only examine or talk about the recollection of dreams. Possibly the recollection of dreams does not correspond directly to them. A great writer of the XVII century, Sir Thomas Browne, thought that our recollection of dreams was much poorer than the splendid reality of them. Others, on the other hand, think that we improve our dreams; that is, if we think our dreams are works of fiction (and I believe so) we will probably continue to imagine as we wake up and later when we tell about our dreams.

– Jorge Luis Borges (1899-1990)

Introduction

The myths that we hold about our dreams are insipid compared to the mythology and spirit revealed in dreams. From time immemorial, people have looked to dreams in fear or hope to foretell the future and guide the dreamer. In antiquity, it was believed that dreams were messages sent by God. There have always been a few extraordinary people who were sought as dream interpreters. Dream stories in the Bible have moral connotations.

To speak of dreams as if they were all one class of marvelous phenomena is as foolish as to discount them all as rubbish. Nobel laureate Francis Crick, physicist and discoverer of DNA, wrote that dreams were like waste being processed or like garbage that should be ignored and discarded. Pure scientists view dreams as manifestations of superstition, magic, and occult phenomena. Psychoanalysis, despite its efforts, has never made the case for being a science.

Contemporary deification of science is a new mythology ruthlessly discounting nonscientific points of view. Yet in this scientific era, supernatural phenomena are increasingly popular in films, theater, song, television, and fiction. Poets, artists, and dreamers conjure up their own truths to spin out-of-this-world experiences.

The Naskapi Indians of Labrador, Canada, live in small nomadic tribes or communities. Their lives depend on the food they hunt. If they did not find food, they starved to death. Their chosen leader relied upon his dreams to direct them to the land where the animals were. The dream was their guiding star.[1]

Growing numbers of people are fascinated by the dream world. From psychological scholars and analysts to spontaneous groups and cults, the dream has a compelling voice. Is it possible that dreams, nightmares, and visions have assumed urgent power because of the dawn of thermonuclear bombs? The decision to drop the atomic bomb out of the heavens was supposedly made and defended by rational arguments such as how many American lives it would save by killing a certain number of Japanese people – a sort of self-evident equation based on a value judgment weighing the numbers of two different classes of presumed human corpses. Destruction was salvation. Perhaps this intellectual argument was the right one, but another type of argument will never end about whether the action was right or wrong. There is an inescapable uncertain moral factor in that decision.

Religious scholars and ecclesiastical and academic authorities build cases for moral decisions on scripture, history, philosophy, biography, and the like. Scientists attempt to frame their works in value-free objective purity – an academic daydream based on the elimination of all dependent variables that would jeopardize the outcome.

I find that many dreams and nightmares of ordinary people are commentaries on morals, values, and ethical judgments – and I should add that abused indefinable concept *family values*. Usually there is that Jungian "light at the core of darkness." From every corner of the world we hear of horrifying atrocities, genocide, and massacres. To survive, people follow political leaders, dictators, generals – tyrants who dare

[1] The Montagnais-Naskapi Indians are nomadic hunters in Labrador who believe that the animals needed for survival must be revealed in dreams and visions. Each hunter depends on his own dream revelations and [there is] nothing others can do to aid in his survival. Game is so scarce that only two or three families are able to hunt together during the long winter. The oldest man in the group is the leader and his dreams gain insight and power with increasing experience in the ways of the animal.

not submit to self-examinations out of fear of being transformed into brooding, indecisive Hamlets.

Experience tells me that it is a dead certainty that monsters dream of hell. Despite the inhuman appearance of perpetrators of evil, they are human like us – and that is the worst nightmare. No major power politician would want to broadcast an unheroic dark side or the fact of seeing a dream analyst. If these things leaked out, the politician's sanity would be judged as insane.

The hope of the world, I believe, rests in ordinary people becoming enlightened, educated, and healthy by not rejecting the wisdom of the dream in making moral judgments.

I intend to make the point in this book that our dreams are our most creative inner source of wisdom and hope. If dreams are such priceless treasures, their understanding should not be limited to the authority of the professionals (a moral judgment). It is a basic Jungian assumption that our dreams serve the purpose of balancing and correcting our conscious attitudes and opinions. Nonetheless, from long experience, when I refer people to therapists who will interpret their dreams, I send them off saying, "Good luck." There is more than meets the ear in that salutation.

I present my basic dream data as evidence, not proof, of my hypothesis. I acknowledge that my selection is neither random nor unbiased. It includes my dreams, and those of my patients who have given me permission to use them. The criterion for selection is simply that each one illustrates a common human life experience that all readers have had or are likely to have.

The dreams relate to normal life crises, such as birth, adolescence, love, marriage, children, illness, and death. The dream narratives are presented as evolving drama as they unfolded in my presence, with my commentaries as listener. Some distracting dream ramifications have been edited. I readily acknowledge an emotional factor in picking one dream from among many because it appealed to me.

This kind of selection process brought to mind the story of a man who walked to work every day passing an iron railing surrounding a large orphanage. One day, he heard a voice cry out to him, "Daddy!" He turned to see a small boy holding onto the railing with both hands, his face pressed between them. In the playground behind him there were many other orphans. The passing man adopted that little boy. The director of the orphanage told him that the child had been at the railing for weeks calling out, "Daddy."

My intention in writing this book is to convey the enormous power of the dream narrative and to present a dramatist way of retelling the story of selected dreams presented in dialogue with me as analyst. I have no particular interest in selling Jungian, Freudian, or any other method of dream analysis, But I draw on my experience of once having been a Freudian analyst and later becoming a Jungian analyst. I am reporting these dreams as if they were literature and not clinical case studies. It would be a pity if dream work were to fade away from professionals or to fall into the mishmash of the dilettante or to be viewed through high-powered lenses of the microscopes of those scientists who believe in just the facts – a narrow view.

I am fully aware that the majority of Americans have no interest in dreams, and are suspicious of what they have heard. I am writing for people who are curious about human nature in all its ramifications and wonders, good and bad. If you react with the feeling, "But I don't have those kinds of dreams," I ask you, "How do you know that?"

When I assume the mission of ferreting out moral issues in dreams, I am aware that I have already assumed a moral position – that is, I am posing an unanswerable question: "Is my hypothesis that dreams can help one make moral decisions right or wrong?" Only in the court of law or logic can one be forced to answer a question – right or wrong, yes or no. Therefore, I remind myself of the following advice by Huanchu Daoren from *Back to Beginnings: Reflections on the Tao*: "Don't be too severe in criticizing people's faults; consider how much they can bear. Don't be lofty in enjoining virtue, so people may be able to follow."

Harry Wilmer
Salado, Texas

Part I
Power

Certain exceptional dreams ... are so imperatively significant, so vitally important, that it would be wrong to withhold them from the knowledge of those who happened not to dream them, and I feel some such quality in my dreams, so strongly that I could scarcely forgive myself if I do not, however briefly, impart them.

– William Dean Howells (1895)

Obedience:

Following Orders

In critical times, our security generally depends on discipline, control, and obedience. This structure is obvious in military and quasi military organizations like the police, firefighters, CIA, FBI, and security forces whose missions involve life and death emergencies. The psychological elements are control, power, and conflict.

Conflicts of interest can undermine the powers needed to make moral and ethical decisions. This problem is clear in the allegiances of the spy. A child's relationship with a parent can create a mire of dominance/submission so that the child, unable to make decisions, has no alternative but to obey and follow orders – one way or another. Individual autonomy is fractured between conscious and unconscious allegiances.

There is an important category of dreams that focuses on authority, from authoritarianism to benevolent authority, and the story plot relates to obedience, following orders, or defying the power of outer authority. A frequent dream image of authority is the police officer.

Understanding the drama helps the dreamer to make a moral and ethical decision. I am not speaking of intellectual insights, but of useful guiding principles for making practical, real-life, moral/ethical decisions. I take a pragmatic point of view and do not enter the grand debates of labels about whether dreams have intentionality, or teleological meaning.

People who hold unyielding or strong conscious beliefs and opinions, who cannot tolerate ambiguity and uncertainty, would find little of value in my approach. I see dream life as a manifestation of our *Weltanschauung* – world view or philosophy of life. This way may lead us to a place where we can understand ourselves in new and strange ways. It may show us how we are being thrown off course and what dangers lurk ahead. Also, it can suggest which direction looks good, and what the hopeful and helpful visions are in our minds.

Dreams rarely tell us exactly what is going to happen, or what to do. Whatever molecular biologic, genetics, or brain function is associated with dreaming, there is an equally important parallel subjective phenomenon in our humanity. This occurrence could be like a message from an inner ancient wisdom, a somewhat obscure oracle, or creative genius trying desperately to get our attention.

I will give each dreamer in the book a pseudonym and disguise identifying details. To illustrate dreams of obedience and following orders, I present a woman who had been long tormented by indecision about which of two men she wanted to choose for a husband. This patient I call Donna. The details of her life are less immediately important than her ambivalence that carries a sense of failure no matter which lover she chooses. She came to see me depressed by life circumstances and an oppressive, rejecting early family life.

In spite of being a prisoner of her childhood, Donna has a strong ego, supports herself, and leads an outwardly successful life. She is attractive. Convinced that she is doomed to lonely isolation and rejection, Donna follows her inner unyielding shadow authority with slavelike obedience. Her life predicament symbolizes the *slave/slave driver* archetype. Donna's inner slave driver symbolizes her mother and the slave dealer, her father. The immorality and suffering in a slave/slave driver human relationship demands extraordinary action, but she was paralyzed in her mind.

It took me months to comprehend the magnitude of the unconscious power she projected onto her rejecting and now powerless parents. It seemed to me that her doom was not that either choice she made would result in failure but that she would never be emancipated and free to make independent, autonomous decisions.

This dream story is about murder, disobedience, and liberation from tyranny.

> **Prologue:** *As the dream begins, I know that I am acting under orders from the CIA or FBI to stop another person from getting involved. I must get power over this person, and keep that person contained. The other person is not identifiable. There are no CIA or FBI officers visible anywhere.*

The dream opens establishing Donna's identity as an agent of the major intelligence agencies responsible for national and international security. The assigned task of the dream is to contain and stop the dangerous other. Intelligence demands thinking and sensation functions, which are her strong conscious characteristics. Their opposite and unconscious functions, feeling and intuition, are underdeveloped and therefore valued less.

Donna must obey orders because if she does not, she endangers the whole (family) system for which she works. She must stop another person from getting involved. To do so, she must get power over "this person," whom I presume is another part of herself who can be dangerous.

If this plot idea is correct, the dream must show the dreamer a decision. Is Donna acting the right way as an intelligence officer? Does the dream suggest that the right way is strictly following orders from the investigating organization? Does it follow that if Donna does not stop the involvement, she will never free herself from the horns of her dilemma?

The dream continues:

I am standing over a man, pouring flour over his head until
he is totally covered with white flour. I don't know why I
should try to stop, because he doesn't seem dangerous. I
leave and go home, take a shower, and get dressed in a pretty
gown preparing to go back to him to have sexual inter-
course. But when I get back, he is dead. He had been killed
by the FBI or CIA because he was a spy.

Donna commented to me, "I had no clear picture of the
man's face, and there was no indication of how he had been
killed. But I knew he was a leader of a spy ring. He had been
killed by my group. I don't know what sort of container held
the flour, but the man looked very conspicuous as if a shroud
or veil had been thrown over a ghost. As I dumped the flour on
him, I felt as if I were having fun like a child."

The dream incorporated the two top powerful national
security agencies that stand for investigative spying and quick
response decisions. The downfall of the spy or police officer
comes when he or she becomes emotionally – sexually –
involved. Donna is ordered to stop involvement, but she
disobeys when she kisses the man over whom she has been
playfully dumping flour. He represents some dead (white
shroud) seductive ghost from her past. Donna loses disci-
plined control and on an impulse decides to kiss him.

He who looks harmless and attractive must be killed. When
Donna returns to seduce him, she finds that her higher powers
have killed him. The members of her group have done their
duty and hers by killing the ghost of her past. The bland affect
of the dream is totally out of keeping with the melodramatic
narrative.

Did Donna's dream help her make a moral decision? Yes,
this dream and other realizations that followed helped her
make her decision, and act.

The manifest dream says that Donna, in not obeying orders,
is disregarding her intelligent agency. On the deepest level of
authority or moral judgment, one might invoke the command-
ment, "Thou Shalt Not Kill." The dream story line, however,

exonerates the killing since that is the legitimate right of the police organizations to whom she has declared allegiance.

More precisely, what is the dream showing her about making a moral decision? The dream was telling her that she should not pay so much attention to her feelings – eros and relationship functions – but rather use her head, her intelligence, her brains. She is not taking her task seriously enough, and is presumably frightened because the haunting ghost of the past could destroy or kill her

Many dreams tell us to follow our feelings when we are snowed under by our brains, but this one warns her that her feelings are out of control. She dreams of action-oriented behavior, not inner reflection and analysis.

The dream was affirming. The end was the necessary completion of the drama. There is an early scene in a play ("I must get power over this man ... ") that is called *scène à faire* which demands a final scene (the killing of the dangerous other in a good guy/bad guy scenario.

Perhaps it is a warning not to decide anything impulsively, for the kiss of death could be fatal to her. From one perspective, it could be said that one part of us must die to enable another part to live.

The Violent Inner Life of a Frightened Woman:

"Assassin in the House!"

A shy, intelligent woman was preoccupied by fears of aging and a lonely, uncertain future. I will call her Ginger. She was eager to tell me a nightmare that had a frightening impact. The aggressive nature of the story was the very opposite of Ginger's mild, adapting nature. Ginger was so intimidated by authority that any thought or deed that smacked of defiance was followed by great anxiety and feelings of guilt.

After several years of analysis, Ginger changed her attitudes toward authority. Tormented by lifelong doubts and dependency needs, she endured each brave new step that caused her to doubt herself. Ginger was outwardly optimistic and charming. Her therapy and dream messages helped her assert her opinions and criticism of women in power. This behavior astonished and pleased her close friends, most of whom were also trying to extricate themselves from masculine and cultural tyranny. Ginger was not yet able to stand up to a man in power, however.

After a striking episode of speaking up to a woman, she had this dream:

> *I am in a strange and dangerous situation in a house or institution. The prominent woman in the house has been handed a threatening note by an unknown woman whose face she did not see. I am trying to help the woman find out the identity of the menacing lady. It seemed apparent that*

the prominent woman had committed some offense, and
that there was going to be a terrible consequence.

The opening scene sets the mood of serious danger about to happen. The lady who delivers the message was seen but could not be identified. She represented dangerous shadow people who should not be disturbed because they have the power of retribution. They are the shadow side of authority, including that of the dreamer. In what form will the announced danger appear? The monster must appear following the opening *scène à faire* that mandates a follow-up on the threat.

The dream continues:

A man comes into the room. He takes out a revolver and
orders everyone to sit in a certain part of the room. They are
hostages. As other people come into the room, he holds
them hostage, too. Then the woman who delivered the
message, whom I was trying to identify, came into the
room. I tried to signal and warn her, but the gunman
caught her. At this point, in some mysterious way, I escaped
from the room.

The real danger appeared as a man taking hostages at gunpoint. People are being used by him for some ulterior dark reason. He is a killer and it seemed as if the threatened woman was the target.

At this critical point, Ginger attempts to protect the messenger who has appeared as a menace, suggesting a bond between the dreamer and the messenger. Both are in mortal danger. The big question at this point is, "What was the meaning of Ginger's mysterious escape?" The story calls for her return, since her disappearing act is another *scène à faire*.

The dream continues:

I go to get my gun. I am a detective or police officer. There
was now another woman helping me. Together we go into
the building and walk along a corridor down which a

stream of famous people are coming toward us. I knew that the man with the revolver was in this crowd, some of whom began shouting, "There's an assassin in the house!" With gun drawn, I begin searching the crowd. People who saw my gun thought I was the assassin, so I shouted, "I am a police officer!"

This is a story of confrontations between a woman and a terrorist gunman. The dreamer is asserting power by attempting to identify a threatening woman and then warning her of the danger to herself. Ginger ends up searching for the killer, prepared to kill him after she had suddenly changed character like Superwoman. The messenger and the aggressive police officer both are parts of the unconscious identity of this mild, peaceful old woman. There is also a close identity between the assassin and the police officer. One is the shadow of the other's consciousness.

The dreamer emerges as a protector of public morals and values. The woman with the gun is ready to kill the man. From deep in the unconscious of this timid, mild, gentle woman comes a violent fighter and protector. Her masculine inner self is both police officer and assassin. A showdown is about to happen.

What makes the melodrama so real is that there is no given end. Like life itself, it is an unfinished story.

Prophetic Dream

Abraham Lincoln held that any dream had value and meaning, and sought clues from his dreams. He believed that the best dream interpreters were the common people with their collective wisdom, whom he called "the children of nature." In the second week of April, 1865, he told the following dream at the White House dinner table to his wife and several guests, including his longtime friend, Colonel A. Ward Lamon, who kept a detailed diary. It is reported in Carl Sandburg's book *Abraham Lincoln: The Prairie Years and the War Years*.

Part I: Mourners Sobbing in the White House

About ten days ago I retired very late. I had been waiting for important dispatches from the front. I could not have long been in bed when I fell into a slumber, for I was weary. I soon began to dream. There seemed to be a deathlike stillness about me. Then I heard subdued sobs, as if a number of people were weeping. I thought I left my bed and wandered downstairs. There the silence was broken by the same pitiful sobbing, but the mourners were invisible. I went from room to room; no living person was in sight, but the same mournful sounds of distress met me as I passed along. It was light in all the rooms. Every object was familiar to me, but where were all the people who were grieving as if their hearts would break?

Part II: Assassination of the President

I was puzzled and alarmed. What could be the meaning of all of this? Determined to find the cause of a state of things so mysterious and so shocking, I kept on until I arrived at the East Room, which I entered. There I met with a sickening surprise. Before me was a catafalque, on which rested a corpse wrapped in funeral vestments. Around it were stationed soldiers who were acting as guards; and there was a throng of people, some gazing mournfully upon the corpse, whose face was covered, others weeping pitifully.

"Who is dead in the White House?" I demanded of one of the soldiers.

"The President," was his answer. "He was killed by an assassin!"

Then came a loud burst of grief from the crowd, which awakened me from the dream. I slept no more that night and although it was only a dream, I have been strangely annoyed by it ever since.

Lincoln then quoted *Hamlet* to Lamon: "To sleep; perchance to dream! Ay, there's the rub."

A few days later on April 14, Lincoln was shot at Ford's Theater.

Another Prophetic Dream

President Lincoln at a meeting of his cabinet told his advisers of another dream he had had the night before, reported by Julien Green in the book *God's Fool: The Life and Times of Francis of Assisi:*

> *I saw myself in a boat, floating over the high seas without oars, without rudder, over a lifeless ocean. There is no one to help. I am drifting, drifting, drifting.*

"But gentlemen," he said, "this has nothing to do with our work. Let's see the business of the day."

Four hours later he was killed at Ford's Theater when John Wilkes Booth fired his revolver.

Learning from Our Animal Natures:

The Cat and the Jackass

In America, ambition, greed, ruthlessness, being on top – number one, and winning constitute our *modus operandi*. It could be said that this is how we make our living. Worldwide, power is equated with rank, money, and impressive possessions. The danger to the powerful winners is that the less powerful defeated people are anxious to change places.

When we are thwarted and feel inferior, our darkest thoughts of resentment, envy, and revenge come to us. At the core of the power problem, fear smolders. The fear of the oppressed becoming the oppressors makes those in power feel justified in brutality, ruthlessness, torture, violence, destruction, and killing. This cruelty is evil.

The dark side of the American psyche is found in our obsession with bigness, loudness, outlandishness, and selfishness, while the bright side of our psyche is generosity, kindness, love, and compassion. It is passion for power that is poisoning politicians. Where is our hope? Is it in reason?

Think about the de Tocqueville quote at the beginning of this book: "In times when passions are beginning to take charge of the conduct of human affairs, one should pay less attention to what men of experience and common sense are thinking than to what is preoccupying the imagination of dreamers." You might consider dream narratives as corrective psychic lenses to sharpen our perception of moral and ethical issues.

The seventeenth-century French philosopher and mathematician Blaise Pascal wrote, "The heart has its reasons which
reason cannot know" (*Pensées IV*). The tragedy is that people
most in need of the wisdom of the heart believe in their own
reason. If one cannot tolerate uncertainty, self-questioning,
and the opposite point of view, then dreams and dreamers are
useless. This condemnation seems to result in frightening
dreams and nightmares in a desperate attempt to get their
attention.

Let us contemplate the dream of a tough old Texan who
ruled his big ranch with an iron grip. The rancher had a deep
affection for his horses, and admiration and respect for his
self-willed donkeys. He loved his cats and dogs. Because of a
horrible drought, he was close to losing his ranch, and he
became depressed for about a month when he woke up from
a dream, laughing. That morning, he became aware that his
depression had evaporated. To him, it was an epiphany:

Our Animal Nature Takes Over

*I fear some disaster is about to happen. I call a meeting of
my family, cowboys, and ranch hands to explain my plan to
meet the danger. When I finish, everyone sits stone silent.
To my surprise, a young ranch hand whom I have just hired
takes over running the meeting. I think, "This is the big put-
down." I become depressed and incapable of taking charge.
My family sits around passively. Their blank, pale faces
remind me of plaster of Paris masks. I think, "My God, these
are my troops!" I become furious, stand up, and shout at
the young ranch hand, "Get the hell out of here!"*

*All the people disappear, leaving my ordinarily docile cat
sitting on a chair in the corner, and a large donkey standing
in the middle of the room. The cat suddenly charges at the
donkey like a ferocious wildcat on a kill. I think the cat has
gone crazy. The donkey runs out the front door. Then the cat
slowly walks back to his chair.*

The old man came to tell me his dream apologetically because his depression was gone. Yet he had a strong need to convey that good news. He had consulted me some years ago about his Vietnam War nightmares.

He began by telling a story to illustrate the tremendous impact of his dream: A rancher could not get his stubborn donkey to move. After all of his usual methods failed, he picked up a two-by-four and cracked the donkey over the head so hard that the animal fell down unconscious. A man standing nearby asked him why he had done that. The rancher replied, "First, I had to get his attention."

The rancher and I came to the conclusion that both the stubborn jackass and the wild cat represented a conflict of forces within himself. His depression brought him down into his unconscious where he experienced a dream. It was a story about the great power of the small, and the realization that it was necessary for him to mobilize the necessary strength to overcome his mood. If he did not, he would be just a stubborn jackass going nowhere.

The Pleaser:

Women Who Must Perform for Men

A beautiful married woman devoted her energies, and in a sense her life, to fulfill her husband's image of the ideal wife. He was a Texas oilman. Her outer rewards and pleasure came from their material possessions, jet-set travel, and social prestige. She had, her husband said, all that a woman could want. He prided himself on his handsome masculine image. His wife dressed in elegant style and spent much time looking at herself in mirrors. Their pictures were featured in the society pages of newspapers and magazines.

Suddenly her husband lost a fortune in the Texas oil bust. Yet they still maintained appearances, thanks to the money his mother gave him. He began to drink. She continued to try to please, flatter, and bolster him, maintaining all the necessary pretense until she became depressed. Afraid that they would lose everything, she saw the shallowness of a life given up to serve a heretofore powerful man. They both felt broken. There were bad arguments. She came to see me because of depression. Her husband ridiculed psychological help because it was for the weak people who would not help themselves.

She told me the following dream shortly after starting psychotherapy:

A Bird in a Gilded Cage

Prologue: *I am traveling on a bus with many people. We are going through a city where all the trees are barren. It is a hot, humid summer day. I get off the bus at a large old Victorian house that I thought was my home. As I approach the building, it becomes a public school. It has a high front gate with bronze bars shaped like spears. I climb up on the gate and look down on the school. As I do this, I drop my zippered handbag, and am afraid that the mirror inside might have broken.*

The metaphor of this opening is clear: She finds herself in a collective situation on a crowded bus – people without limousines. The barren trees are the trees of winter in summertime. Her Victorian image of her house (herself) becomes a public school in which children learn. When she looks down on it, she drops her pocketbook. This incident was the downfall of her wealthy identity, and might have broken her vanity mirror. That is her situation the day of the dream. It is not a feeling of gloom and danger, but rather one of becoming less outstanding, less glamorous. At the end of the prologue, there is a paradoxical situation – dropping both her identity (cards) and femininity, symbolized by her purse. From her precarious perch, she drops her old identity as the pleasing woman and could have broken her old mirror.

We can assume that the story will go on to amplify the unpredictable situation, and show us whether the psyche expects bad or good things to happen. Will hope or despair dominate?

The dream continues:

I see an empty plastic birdseed holder that fits into a bird cage. On the top of the seed holder is a bas-relief of the corpulent smiling Buddha looking very peaceful. There is a ring holder on the Buddha and I thought I could use it for a pendant to hang around my neck.

In the dream, I think that I must tell you, Harry, about the possible broken mirror and the Buddha I could wear as a necklace. Suddenly a streetwise man appears and tells me, "Don't follow the man down the steps into the musty basement."

As the song goes, "Who Could Ask for Anything More?" The seed holder is empty. Yet while the material food is not there for feeding the bird, symbolic of the caged spirit, an ancient spiritual symbol appears on top of the feeder. The smiling Buddha is the emblem of the Self – peaceful repose and compassion. This figure can be worn as an amulet to ward off suffering and evil While the vanity mirror that reflects outer life might be broken, the Buddha is a smiling representation of enlightenment.

Siddhartha, son of a wealthy father, lived a wildly indulgent life. He had all the material treasures that would assure him of a princely life, but he chose to renounce that life for poverty. In the end, he found enlightenment while meditating under a bo tree. He became Buddha, who taught, according to Bukkyo Dendo Kyokai: "The secret of health for both mind and body is not to mourn for the past, not to worry about the future, or not to anticipate troubles, but to live wisely and earnestly for the present."

After the wife of the oilman discovers a Buddha with the ring holder, a streetwise man appears to warn her not to follow that man who was descending the steps into the dark musty basement. The man who might lead her into the dark basement represents her husband in decline.

The dream continues:

I feel I should go down with him, and I feel hurt that he is going without me. The streetwise man says, "I don't believe you should do that. Just be yourself." I see a corridor down below and on each side is a row of prison cells. At the bottom doorway, I can see a woman slumped in a chair in the morning light. I wake up feeling good.

She Who Must Be Right

Will Admit No Error

The Pleaser's dark sister is She Who Must Be Right, who is intent on displeasing the other. In Jungian terms, she is the opinionated animus with whom a man can never win an argument, and to whom reason or contrary opinions hold no water. Her relationship to other women ranges from the Absolute Authority to Flatterer, who ingratiates by having no opinion of her own. She acts as if the other woman is always right, and convinces herself of it for some benefit.

With She Who Must Be Right, a man-friend (lover or husband who brings her gifts) will find, almost without exception, that they are not the right ones. That is a moral dilemma. For him, to be good is to be bad. The man is forbidden to take the role of the Pleaser. This situation inevitably leads to mutual anger, rejection, and lingering bitterness. The man can only win the argument – be right by being silent – after stating his opinion.

Such action is not being a coward, but being intelligent enough not to get into a fight that is impossible to win. It is characteristic of this kind of relationship behavior that the woman must have the last word. She is in a state of mind that can admit no error. She herself is helpless to do so.

The opposite animus archetype is symbolized in the woman upon whom the man projects his idealized anima of love, the ultimate pleaser. The heroine in Rider Haggard's book *She*, called She Who Must Be Obeyed, is the most beautiful woman in the world, the eternal feminine spirit, overpowering, and irresistibly attractive. Jung used this story as an example of the anima archetype.

It is important for me not to speculate on the psychology of this behavior because my opinion will probably be wrong. I shall remain silent and invoke the wisdom of a woman's dream:

My Mother Was Always Right:
I Must Admit My Error

A woman whom I will call Jenny said that she had a right to blame her mother for her shame, failure, and self-doubt. Jenny cited as evidence that she had never had a reasonable, loving relationship with her mother, and childhood was marked by her mother's domination and a depressed father who could please neither mother nor daughter. No matter what the father or patient said or did, it was wrong in her mother's eyes. She called her mother mean, and she was still enraged and furious at her.

Jenny came to me to try to straighten out her mother problem. Intelligent and savvy, Jenny knew in her mind that to continue blaming someone else for one's problems leads nowhere. Blaming becomes demonic. That insight did not stop her hatred and blame, however. She really came to me expecting some miraculous change.

The dream starts out:

> *I am back home as a child. My mother leaves the house wearing a fur coat even though it is a terribly hot summer day. I don't want her to go, but she gets into her car and starts to drive off, leaving me. I am so enraged with my mother that just as she is passing me, I take the pencil I am holding in my hand and start stabbing the window on the driver's side. It makes holes in the glass but does not shatter it. I want to hurt my mother, who speeds off leaving me lying in the dirt street. As the car is going by, I grab at the*

back bumper trying to hold the car back, but I am left lying
flat on my back. I was so angry I could have killed my
mother.

This dream began with a big dramatic opening scene of fury
at a mother who has no feeling for her. The fur coat suggests
the mother's irrationality. Her person is being guarded by
dead animal persona. The mother is all wrapped up in the
shadow of herself. There was no way Jenny could reach her
mother, whether through love or violence. All Jenny could do
was to pull herself up out of the dirt and stand on her own two
feet.

It is as if the dream says to let go of her mother in life and
fantasy because Jenny is unable to cope with the overpowering force of the mother archetype. Will the dream now offer
her some clue that will help the clinging, unwanted daughter
to disarm her mother threat?

The dream continues:

An old woman dressed in very ordinary clothes appears. She
cleans me up and takes me to her home, saying, "I am going
to hide you from danger." The old woman hires a very
smart, pretty, young woman lawyer to defend me.

Jenny finds encouragement in the dream. The plain old
woman represents a protecting and holding (in her home)
mother figure. Jenny is the special and only child of this
caring woman. The magnitude of the danger is indicated by
the need to hide her. Jenny associates this notion with families
who hid Jews from the Nazis. The dream suggests that the
danger is the return of the mother. The old woman bolsters
Jenny with a special lawyer who symbolizes the patient's ego
ideal – all that Jenny longed to be.

There is an important point in the interpretation of this
dream that I believe is a major question in dream analysis. A
helpful woman protector and guide appears when Jenny is
down and brings her to her own secure place where there is

help by a previously unknown woman who represents her wished-for mother. This woman shows Jenny a new strong young helper who already exists within her. Does the helping, nonspecific, previously unknown helper represent the analyst or the patient? What assurance can one have that this dream represents transference to the analyst?

This is a crucial question. The fact that this figure is a woman is irrelevant because any analyst can be imagined as mother, father, and the like.

I propose that it is an unwarranted stretch of the imagination and an ego-driven intrusion of classical psychoanalytic theory to identify the rescuing woman as myself. When analysts make such interpretations, their analysands generally see enough elements of truth in them that they don't contradict the analyst's authority and say, "No, it isn't you. It is me." The overriding point is that taking credit diminishes the patient.

Therefore, I see the plain woman as the image of the patient's inner helpful, caring, powerful mother. She is the mirror opposite of how Jenny sees her other mother. She is the symbol of hope for the patient. To recognize the image as a part of herself means that she is her own "inner analyst" whom she always carries within herself wherever she is. The symbol is capable of bringing out Jenny's inner idealized woman of unsuspected beauty and youthful energy.

I think the dream suggests that the angry attack on the image of her mother seen through the glass is pointless and ineffectual. The presence of a pencil in her hand is not a weapon of destruction, but rather one of creation. It stands for the patient's considerable writing talent to be used for the right reasons. That is a moral decision.

With all the positive potentials thus identified, how will the dream end – as a magical story in which everything is resolved or as some unexpected danger?

> **Epilogue:** *I am lost in a large parking lot, wandering around in it. Suddenly some wild young people come rushing at me, to attack me just because I am there.*

This final two-sentence commentary suggests a variety of meanings:

(1) Jenny is not yet out of danger.

(2) The attack occurs without any rational explanation.

(3) It happens just because she is there. To me, that metaphor suggests the hand of fate – which strikes as it is, where and when it will. She had the mother and father she did just because they were both there at the time of her conception. Each one of us gets the parents who are given to us.

(4) At the time of the dream, Jenny is still lost and wandering and must now face her own shadow images of the murderer. That is the problem in the parking lot.

(5) The dream as a whole implies that she can now survive if she uses her newfound inner strength.

Notes

1. Moffitt, Kramer, and Hoffman in their book *The Functions of Dreaming* present a diverse collection of modern views of this perennial question by theoreticians, researchers, and practitioners of the human and life sciences, but without any contribution from the humanities.

2. There is a certain power that exists in drama and narrative, while the power of story itself enhances the power of its ideas. Almond and Almond, both therapists, have written a book about the therapeutic process, fictional relationships, and the process of psychological change drawn from nine significant novels. They refer to the therapeutic narrative in psychoanalysis. Few references are made to dreams except to explain that both in novels and psychoanalysis there are manifest and latent meanings. For example, they call *The Magus* by John Fowles "a literary psychodrama." The authors view the novel from three perspectives: reality events, transference fantasies, and dreams. The book is not about dreams in novels, and

devoted only a few paragraphs to the dream concept and not to dreams in the novels, but rather about how the dream concept can be applied to literature.

3. I have addressed the dream in my article "Psychiatrist on Broadway," where I singled out Moss Hart's 1941 musical hit "Lady in the Dark" as the only Broadway play up to 1955 that ever presented an intelligent, well-balanced psychoanalyst analyzing a patient's dreams. This drama contrasted with "The Dream Doctor," a grotesquely vilifying play that started the psychiatric era on Broadway in 1922.

Anne Hudson Jones in her chapter "Psychiatrists on Broadway" (1974-1982) wrote of five plays in which only one, "Duet for One" (1982), portrayed a strong, intelligent, competent psychoanalyst. The therapy failed, the play bombed, and there were no dreams analyzed.

4. As an analyst, I have been keenly aware of the literary and narrative capacity of therapists and patients in relating their case material as story. I have also observed that the same analysts dramatize themselves to dramatize their cases. Others with more professional (and compulsive) writing skills report boring case material. Currently there is a growing literature in analysis on the subject of the narrative.

When I think of presenting dreams as straight drama, I recall the stage manager/narrator in Thornton Wilder's Pulitzer Prize-winning popular play "Our Town." If I were making such a play, the stage manager would come out at the curtain opened and narrate the prologue. In a sense, that is what I have done in the text of this book.

5. James Hillman, writing on case history as fiction, said that "psychoanalysis is a work first of all with imaginative tellings and that therefore we must regard it as an activity in the realm of *poesis*, which I take to mean making by imagination into words." Hillman proceeds to explain Freud's fiction writing in this way:

> His psychoanalysis could make no further headway in the world at which he aimed it, medicine, unless he could find a suitable form of "telling" that gave the conviction, if not the substance, of medical empiricism. Freud tangled the two because he was engaged in both at once: fiction and case history; and ever since then in the history of our field, they are inseparable, even if we, engaged in this field, have lost touch with this double fact, this duplicity (which Freud did not), that our cases are a way of writing fiction.

Hillman notes one of Freud's devices was that of

... the humble narrator in the background compared with the momentousness of what is revealed in his presence and to his reflection; the deepening of discoveries in answer to "what happens next." ... Early on in the taking down of case histories, Freud found that he was not recording a true account of historical events, but fantasies of events as if they actually happened. The material of case history is not historical facts but psychological fantasies, the subjective stuff that is not the proper domain of fiction. ... Case history is a fiction in the sense of an invented account of an imagined interior process of a central character in a narrative story. ...

Where Freud was a writer of fictions, Jung was a writer on fictions. And for Jung, the more fictitious and far-out the better. ... For such "materials" obliged him to meet them on an equally imaginative level. But – both Freud and Jung assumed an empirical posture, subjecting them to empirical criticisms and attempted to reply with empirical defenses. They would have both been better served had they turned for help to the field they are themselves working, the field of literary imagination. ...

Jung said the dream had a dramatic structure, which he noted as statement of place, dramatis personae, culmination or crisis, and solution or lysis. Hillman reacts (the emphasis is mine):

It is instructive, useful – and misleading. For the dramatic structure is not true on the level Jung posits it; the dreams one sees in practice can rarely be discerned into four clear-cut stages, because dreams are mainly abrupt and fragmentary or hysterically swollen and meanderingly long. *Moreover, the dramatic structure is misleading in a deeper sense: The dream is primarily an image –* oneiros *(dream in Greek) means "image" and not "story." We may see the dream narratively, allegorically, or dramatically, but in itself it is an image or group of images. When we see drama in it, we are* always in part *seeing our own hypothesis.*

My reaction to Hillman is that his vision is limited by literal word definition, and such a hypothesis is "always in part" a strange emphasis because it seems self-evident to me that we cannot see dreams without acknowledging that we see them to some degree according to our hypothesis. Hillman, after his exposition of the fiction of history and case material, introduces his own fiction (hypothesis) that because dreams are characterized by images that they cannot be narrative, drama, or story. He would be better served by turning to literary imagination. When we watch a play, we see a sequential series of images, sometimes abrupt, sometimes fragmentary or swollen, and sometimes meanderingly long. I think he is misleading, because the images on stage become a story by action and illusion. Anyone who has written a play knows that when it is produced with director, actors, and setting, it is likely to be a far cry from what the author had in mind. If one can understand dreams in analysis by viewing them in a dramatic motif, to resort to the authority of the Greek word *oneiros* as meaning "image" and not "story" is a tragic proof of a moral decision of which is right, in a theatrical line.

7. C. G. Jung wrote (*CW* 10: Para. 826):

Often the moral judgment is displaced into a dream which the subject does not understand. For example, a businessman I knew made what looked like a pretty serious and honorable offer which, it turned out much later, would have involved him in a disastrous fraud had he accepted it. The following night after he received this offer, which as I say seemed to him quite acceptable, he dreamed that his hands and forearms were covered with black dirt. He could see no connection with the events of the previous day, because he was unable to admit to himself that the offer had touched him on the vulnerable spot: his expectation of a good business deal. I warned him about this, and he was careful enough to take certain precautions which did in fact save him from more serious harm. Had he examined the situation right at the beginning he would undoubtedly have had a bad conscience, for he would have understood it was a "dirty business" which his morality would not have allowed him to touch. He would, as we say, have made his hands dirty. The dream represented this locution in pictorial form. ... In order for him to become conscious of his moral reaction, that is, to feel his conscience, he had to tell the dream to me. This was an act of conscience on his part, insofar as dreams always made him feel a little uncertain.

8. In *God's Fool*, Green writes of the power of dreams:

The psychology of medieval people, who acted so often on premonitions, saw in dreams a divinely chosen method for communicating with them and, at times, for revealing God's will. The same was true of visions. They were mental phenomena, no doubt, but so vividly detailed that people had the certainty they were seeing images outside themselves. In their eyes illusion was impossible and, setting all reason aside, they followed their dreams straight into action. There was no psychoanalysis to disturb this system of dynamic ideas come from another world. For human beings in those distant times, sleep offered a source of spiritual energy and even mystical revelations. Have we changed all that much?

9. Nebuchadnezzar remembered the dream about the tree in the midst of the earth that grew until its top reached heaven. He said, "Hew down the tree" but gave instructions to leave its roots (Daniel 4:14-15). Daniel, dismayed by the meaning of the dream, warned the King that like the tree, he had grown great and special, but because the King regarded himself as author of his power and assumed a godlike role, the Almighty God will cut him down. The dream compensates for Nebuchadnezzar's hubris, but because the King did not heed the warning, he lost his mind in megalomania.

10. A conversation with Jungian analyst Joseph Henderson on February 25, 1996:

Harry: "I am going to give a lecture in San Antonio on 'The Moral Purpose of Dreams.' What do you think when you hear that title?"

Joe: "I wouldn't think they had any moral purpose. That is my first reaction. I would say that they are basically unmoral, because to be moral implies a conscious philosophical point of view."

Harry: "I am not saying that the dream per se is moral, but it is not without moral values. It is an aspect of nature on which we project our moral judgments. The moral purpose of dreams is to give us some opposites upon which we can project moral values. Perhaps that is why there are so many 'right' and 'wrong' ways of interpreting dreams."

Joe: "Of course dreams present opposites and the opposites offer the means of reconciliation, or at least understanding of what the separation of opposites means. It's like everything in the day is good and everything in the night is bad. That's how primitive people are. But we have the same sense in our culture that good and evil present a choice. That's basically Manichaean[1] that there is a good God and a bad God and everything you do good goes to the good one, and everything you do bad goes to the bad one. So there's a kind of insistence of man taking a moral attitude toward the unconscious."

Harry: "Choice involves ethical decisions and conflicts of duty. I think that ethical and moral conflicts in our lives appear in the symbolism of our dreams."

11. C. G. Jung wrote in Volume 8 of his *Collective Works* (Para. 8):

Many people who know something, but not enough, about dreams and their meaning, and who are impressed by their sub-

---

[1] The doctrine of Manichaeism was the conflicting dualism between the realm of God, represented by light and spiritual enlightenment, and the realm of Satan, symbolized by darkness and the world of material things.

tle and apparently intentional compensation, are liable to succumb to the prejudice that the dream actually has a moral purpose, that is, it warns, rebukes, comforts, foretells the future, etc. If one believes that the unconscious always knows best, one can easily be betrayed into leaving the dreams to make the necessary decisions, and is then disappointed when the dream becomes more and more trivial and meaningless. Experience has shown me that a slight knowledge of dream psychology is apt to lead to an overrating of the unconscious which impairs the power of conscious decision. The unconscious functions satisfactorily only when the conscious mind fulfills its task to the very limit. A dream may perhaps supply what is then lacking, or it may help us forward where our best efforts have failed.

12. Science has accomplished almost unbelievable achievements, the most recent being the cloning of sheep in Scotland [*Nature*, 1997; 385: 810-13]. It is only natural consequence that this has created a worldwide debate on the ethics and morality involved, if scientists extend cloning to human beings. We now have a moral dilemma that cannot be resolved. I quote an article from JAMA (*Journal of the American Medical Association*, July 2, 1997, 278/1:13):

> Human cloning should be put on hold – but only temporarily, the National Bioethics Commission concluded in a report issued last month. In a letter transmitting the Bioethics Commission report [which the president had asked to be delivered within ninety days] to the White House, Harold T. Shapiro, president of Princeton University, ... said there is a need for a "great deal more widespread education and deliberation to resolve the legal and moral issues involved."

JAMA commented:

> His remarks emphasized the concern that the members of the commission expressed repeatedly during the eight meetings the group held to prepare their report. While they found the idea of cloning humans repugnant, neither did they like the idea of restricting scientific inquiry, and the report does not pretend to have resolved the moral issues involved.

Even the thought (read: *fantasy*) that a government commission in Washington, D.C., could *ever* resolve the moral issues in this case is incredulous. Ethical and legal issues may be resolved for now, but the moral issues will never be resolved. The commission reported, "Neither moral philosophers nor religious thinkers can agree on the 'best' moral theory." Of course, there is no best moral theory. To claim a best moral theory would be immoral. The analytic psychologist is in no better position on the morals of the issue than the postal clerk.

> 12. *The moral of the dream is not in the dream.*
> *Why moralize? Why not make up your own mind?*
> *Never say "never." There is no moral in the dream.*
> *Never say "always." There is no moral in the dream*
> *Because you will find it when you wake up dreaming*
> *If you really need it.*
> *It does you no good while you're sleeping –*
> *OOPS! – I should never say that again*
> *Because it probably is not true.*
>
> – Harry Wilmer

13. Hillman concludes his book *Healing Fiction* with this paragraph:

> For the whole therapeutic opus with its vision of perfection in the love of fellow-feeling can never leave the tiny beginning, the bit of gravel in the shoe, the *petit tache humide* that returns us to feelings of inferiority which are given embodiment in our organic creatureliness. And so, even our answers to "What does the soul want?" do not put us on top of the question. We are not coming out all right, *all* shall be well. We are, however, attempting to remain in touch with the soul by means of the question. For psychotherapy it may be enough to remember not *what* it wants, but *that* it wants, and that the soul's eternal wanting is psychotherapy's eternal question. (p. 129)

The first chapter in this book, on "The Fiction of Case History: A Round," is the same chapter I discussed earlier from another book, in which he contrasts Freud's allegorical fiction of the dream with Jung's metaphorical fiction of the dream, both of which require translation (pp. 35-36).

Hillman states the case of fiction and Jung this way: "Know Thyself in Jung's manner means to become familiar with, to open oneself to and listen to, that is, to know and discern daimons. Entering one's interior story takes a courage similar to starting a novel" (p. 55).

Part II
Evil

Good and evil, we know, in the field of this world, grow up together almost inseparably.

– John Milton
Areopagitica

Thou Shalt Not Kill:

A Mother's Nightmare

The dream:

I have just killed a newborn baby, like it was a victim of a fire but showed no evidence of the fire. It was like the children t Hiroshima. I feel a terrible need to get the baby back to life. I naturally have the feeling that I have done something terrible.

A murdered baby. The appearance of Hiroshima – instant death without marks. Taking on the guilt of the nuclear world. Now the question is, what will happen to the dreamer and the dead baby? Is all irretrievably lost? Is this an apocalyptic dream? I call it evil.

The dream continues:

I am back with the people in the Land of the Dead. The only people who can see the baby are the dead ones. And to them, the baby is alive. I sense that the World of the Dead is malevolent and I can see that they are plotting to kill a man who is the only person there except me who is not dead. I know that I have the power to go back and forth between the World of the Living and the World of the Dead. No one else can see the Dead World unless they are dead. I woke up thinking that I ought to write the dream down, but I also thought that I ought to forget it.

This dream is a grim reminder that the mythological world lives in our collective unconscious. I did not interpret it. I listened to it and wanted to forget it also. In my long experience, I have formed the opinion that it is not productive and may be destructive to analyze this kind of dream in terms of the dreamer's personal life.

Yet the mythology of the World of the Shades and the Underworld, along with the myths of the people who could move between the two worlds – like Persephone and the blind seer Tiresias – help us understand the deepest dimensions of the psyche and add a sense of dignity and collective wisdom to the discussion of the awful elements. While I have placed this dream under the Evil category, its meaning is so poignant that there is literally no possible way to tell you how the dreamer and I discussed this dream.

That dilemma is an insurmountable problem in writing a book about dreams in analysis, and why I have elected to present them in a special format of drama and story. I am not deeply interested in the theoretical and academic formulations because they resonate in my mind as words, words, words, in the brilliance of the minds of thinking people.

The practicing clinical psychoanalyst, psychiatrist, or psychologist who works with dreams is generally quite inept at conveying what happens during analysis. This conclusion – in my mind – eliminates the possibility of there ever being a science of dream subjectivity. Dream objectivity is an artifact and an artificial construct.

Where does this leave me – in the category of art, philosophy, literature, or the humanities? The answer is obvious to me: I don't belong to any category. I never was a Freudian. I never was a Jungian. I am not even a dream analyst. I am not a scientist, although I once was a research pathologist. You have to start listing the qualifications to belong to a designated group. This condition is no dilemma for me. I call myself a Jungian analyst because I have to call myself something, but I am merely Harry Wilmer trying his level best to understand the human condition within the sphere he has chosen.

The Evil Within, the Evil Without:

A Dream Investigation

Many strong and very effective people to whom you relate in your daily life have suffered terrible psychological wounds early in their lives. You would be shocked to know of their early tragedies, abuse, and violence, and the hidden dark thoughts and images that hover in their minds. Friends, acquaintances, and family may be totally unable to understand how such a good person could possibly commit some horrible deed. "He (or she) never caused trouble, was thoughtful and kind, and led an exemplary life," they may say.

Therefore, if the good person becomes the bad person, it is a story of great interest and can usually be found on the front pages of the newspapers or in lead news reports on television – the perfectly normal-appearing person who suddenly runs amok. It is as though the individual is possessed by demons.

In sophisticated intellectual society, we use learned abstract words to protect us from the merciless demon ideas. Naturally, science must investigate the chemistry associated with unusual behavior and thinking. We have drugs that can control disturbing symptoms. Nonetheless, such events are an inherent part of the human drama. Biochemical, physiological, biological, genetic, and molecular investigations are all necessary research areas.

We are also obliged, however, to examine the factors in a person's life history and environment to help account for destructive and self-defeating behavior. Clinical and psychological researches into social, cultural, and moral aspects, childhood development, and dream life are equally important. Investigations of dreams must not be neglected or ignored because some authorities believe that dream research is a blind alley, rather than seeing the blind eye in their own heads.

I am going to tell you about a successful man with extraordinary business and relationship skills. People around him could not see beneath the surface. They were inevitably ignorant of his unconscious, and had no clue as to his dark thoughts or impulses. It is essential to acknowledge that beneath the persona of the observing people lurked the same potential dangers that they must not admit.

With my patient, I did not see or feel a danger of his explosion, provided we continued to investigate his psyche with its strengths and its fragile places. I report one dream that had a powerful impact on his life. It would be foolish to believe that one dream alone could be The Great Liberator, yet it would also be foolish to discount the power of one dream.

The following dream was one in a long series of dreams with which we had worked. I do not overemphasize the importance of my specific interpretations. Countless other interpretations could be made and defended. I know, however, that my attitude toward my patient and his toward me, my careful listening and giving him a model of appreciating his own creative dream life, and my conviction that dreams have a meaning were all strong elements in the success of our work together.

I stress that it is only when my interpretation has a positive reception by my patient that I am content to think that it is right – not the only right one, but a significantly correct interpretation. In the final analysis, it is only the patient's interpretation or corroboration with the therapist's interpretation of the dream that rings a bell.

Each time I listen to a dream, I ask myself, "Can this dream be used to help the dreamer, and if it can, how can it help?" That is my guiding principle.

The Great Investigation

Prologue: *I am in my bedroom where a large wooden wardrobe stands against the wall. I push it aside, exposing a hole in the wall. The edges of the hole are rotten and ugly. I had no idea that there was such severe damage.*

The first scene opens on a hole in the wall that was hidden by furniture. The nature of the margin of the hole suggests that the rotting process has been going on for a long time, finally breaking through as an opening in the wall. Natural curiosity leads the observer to think that the dreamer is next going to look into the hole. What lies deeper into the unforeseen? That is the dream mystery. So far, all we have seen is the set with damage to be explored like an open inner wound.

The dream continues:

Act I: Inner Space

I look into the hole and see a large room that I think is the basement. The strangest thing about the room is that it has no walls. Clustered in the middle of the room are objects that are being stored. I could see the dimension of the room by the floor and realize that I must rebuild the walls, and repair the rotten wall space with Sheetrock. I start working at the job.

An inner problem being repaired by the dreamer has been discovered after passing through the threshold. The objects clustered in the center of the basement are nondescript. Is there something important to know about their contents or do the boxes simply reinforce the idea that what is put below the surface must have walls to contain whatever is put within them? Taken n a metaphoric sense, they contain memories – or objects and images (substantial or insubstantial).

We will do well to stick to the dream's manifest content, and not be carried away by fantasy: The dreamer's attention is focused in on the dream fact that there are no walls. He is given no hint that there had been walls that crumbled or were destroyed. The dream indicates that they have just disappeared.

That is the first mystery for him to reconstruct, and it has the a priori pattern of a three-dimensional container. Psychologically, I imagine that the basement represents the dreamer's unconscious and something has gone wrong down there. As he tells me what he is going to do, I feel it is a good prognostic message for coping with his problems in life.

Up to this point, the dream gives no hint of danger. There are no bad people, no demons. There are no helping hands. There is no plot. The story has elaborated on the setting, but has introduced no heroic theme, no slayer of the dragon – only a casual explorer of the unconscious. The picture of the dreamer putting up Sheetrock and repairing the basement is so positive that it creates a subtle apprehension about an unexpected, negative intrusion.

Act II: Plainclothes Police Arrive on the Scene

About six police investigators arrive. Although they show no badges and wear plain clothes, I know they are police officers. They are a nasty, aggressive lot, fighting with each other. While this takes place in my home, I know that it is also their headquarters. I am both observer and one of them.

What have they come to do? They are messing up my house. Their violence increases. I am not frightened for my life, but I feel the pitch of tension building up. Then I realize that they are terrorists. If they are terrorists, am I one, too? A strange old man arrives with news that time is running out. This means that we must begin our investigation before it is too late.

The dreamer suggests that the strange old man who has come to warn him is Harry Wilmer. I assumed that he is not me, but rather a generic analyst. In that sense, he represents a part of me. To attribute this crucial role to his analyst would have made me personally too central a figure in the dreamer's ability to make a decision. I told the dreamer that the wide old man was the analyst within him. I can say that the archetypal guide is symbolized in both of us, and in innumerable others. That interpretation prevents anyone from getting inflated.

The dreamer associates the warning of the short time in the dream with events of the day before. It is also a cautionary word that speaks to universal life ordeals. The message is clear. It is a good idea to suggest that you pay great attention to any such astonishingly succinct verbal dream messages. They carry an emotional impact and have meaningful clues for moral and ethical decisions.

I remember a powerful personal experience at a troubled time in my life when I was sitting in the Stanford University chapel one evening. Suddenly these words surfaced in my mind: "Things are better than they are." They had a stunning impact because they did not seem to be related to anything. It was as if they had flown right out of the blue, speaking just to me. I knew that I must remember them. They were a profound comment on life itself. These six words came when they were urgently needed, and remind me of the saying in India, "When the student is ready, the guru will appear."

At an anguished time, I received those six words, telling me in effect, "You did the right thing." They had an aroma like ambrosia, and their moral advice was crystal clear: You must not ruminate and obsess about past decisions. You ought not try to rewrite history because you did the right thing at that time, considering what you knew, how things were, and what you did not know at that time. If you acted after thoughtful deliberation and not impulsively, there was no way you could have done anything else but what you did do.

I am not throwing in the "if only" about hindsight, or the cliché, "You did the best you could" (poor chap), but instead making a moral judgment: You did the right thing. This statement implies that any other thing you might have done was the wrong thing at that moment. You may find that at a later date what you did proved to be wrong, but if you can accept the six-word maxim your life will be easier and pleasanter, and you will have given yourself permission to live in the present.

The patient dreamer was still caught in his remote past, wishing it had been different. It could only have been the rage which still simmered in his psyche that continually haunted his life in the present. This realization called for a shattering wake-up call.

Act III: The Terrible Solution

When the anger of the investigators is at its most intense and dangerous pitch, I realize that there is a broken window in the house. I discover that "poison" is being blown in. The police identify the poison and immediately find an antidote. I repair the broken window and realize that this kind of poison had made us crazy. Within a short time, the antidote cures the crazy violence, and we no longer are terrorists. Then we go to carry out our investigation in the basement.

The poison was his anger blowing in from the past outer reality. Anger is being mad. The Greek word *pharmakon* means both "antidote" and "poison." There is a special meaning in these close opposites that relates to medicine, psychology, analysis, and human behavior. That which heals can kill, and vice versa.

In the dream, the police themselves were both criminals and law enforcement officers. A proper use of the right psychology ca neutralize darkness, while a misuse of psychology can poison. The dream tells us a story of an individual, almost at the mercy of his unconscious, who reconstructs his psyche after uncovering its ugly holes. All danger never disappears, but it is heartening to know that we can gain control of our minds. *Control* was the central issue in my patient's life.

The dreamer's moral decision comes after he realizes that he is not trapped in the poisonous terror of the Shadow World. He sees new hope and strength to live in the present. The most remarkable part of his new understanding was that it came from within himself, via his dreams. I could comment on the content of the dreams, but the content was his alone. Focusing on the manifest dream content is the hallmark of Jungian psychology and ignored in classical Freudian psychology which focuses on the so-called "latent dream" that no one ever saw.

His Thoughts Were Not Evil – His Deeds Were Evil:

A Vietnam Story

This is the story of a Vietnam veteran whose dreams and war experiences I listened to and, when possible, analyzed. The Vietnam War, after the My Lai massacre, forced the face of evil onto the American scene. We expect our enemies to do evil deeds, not American troops. However uncharacteristic of the American forces in Vietnam, My Lai was an inescapable fact. We dehumanize our enemy so that our troops can kill them without guilt, but old men and women and children murdered point blank?

The book *Sanctions for Evil* (by Nevitt Sanford, Craig Comstock and associates) addresses the legitimation of evil in war to create a condition for guilt-free massacre. This state is made possible by dehumanizing the enemy and denying the humanity of the civilian victims – men, women, children, and babies. The so-called "guilt-free" state designates the moment of killing. Like all value-free conditions, it is short-lived, or has no real life except for theoreticians.

I worked with 109 war combat Vietnam veterans suffering from posttraumatic stress disorder over a two-year period. I can report that these men often tried to work off their guilt by seeing cold-blooded injustice around them and facing it on their return home. First, most of them felt alienated and shamed by a rejecting society – contempt as baby killers and dope addicts who lost the war. Their military uniforms were painful reminders of a shameful American defeat at the hands of an extremely small country ten thousand miles from home, of which Americans had known practically nothing before a war that was called a "conflict" and not a war. Denial was there from the beginning.

When I lectured to audiences about my study on nightmares of Vietnam combat veterans, it was possible to elicit shock and sympathy but neither empathy nor compassion. At some point in my lecture as I touched on particularly awful events, I suddenly saw that I was speaking to staring, uncomprehending people. They blanked out because my words were a warning of the dangerous, dark parts of everyone's psyche – *every*one's. Americans developed an amnesia for the reality they had seen on the television screens in their own homes.

Survivor's guilt is well known to most people, because in some degree we have all experienced it. American participation in wanton killing, slaughter, mutilation, and torture, however, shattered the illusions of the United States being good, right, and triumphant. Those atrocities are what war propaganda says our enemies do.

Similar denial was characteristic of the reaction of the British and Americans to the German Nazi extermination policies. Arthur Koestler, who lectured to audiences in the early 1940s about this horror, wrote:

> *There is a dream that keeps coming back to me at almost regular intervals; it is dark, and I am being murdered in some kind of thicket or brushwood; there is a busy road at no more than ten yards' distance; I scream for help but nobody hears me, the crowd walks past, laughing and chattering. … I have quarreled about it with analysts, and I believe it to be an archetype in the Jungian sense: an expression of the individual's ultimate loneliness when faced with death and cosmic violence and his inability to communicate the unique horror of his experience.*
>
> *(Sanford, Comstock, et al., p. 60)*

Vietnam 1968

I shall call him George. He was thirty-three years old when he consulted me in 1981, twelve years after his return from Vietnam. He was referred to me because of his war nightmares that were still recurring several time every week and his rage, violence, and inability to adjust to "the world." George was a tall, tough, handsome, muscular man. He exuded a sense of menace and threat. Yet he was courteous, civil, and eager to talk to me.

He did not have much good to say about the Veterans Administration hospital or his previous "shrinks." I told him I wanted to meet with him for a series of talks about his Vietnam experiences, and especially his dreams. I explained that this was part of a study I was conducting and that I wanted his permission to audiotape our talks and use them in a book. George readily agreed. As I do with all of my patients, I asked him to call me Harry.

He started off saying, "Twelve fucking years! Twelve fucking years of mental terror, turmoil, nightmares, and hatred. One moment I love my fellowman, and the next moment I'd just as soon the whole goddamn earth would blow up. 'Go ahead ... start a nuclear war.' If I were just a survivor, then it would be 'Do or die.' You know what I mean? ... The world is a sham, Harry. It's all nothing to me. The real truth never comes out of peoples' mouths. They have a role to play all their lives. They have to be a certain entity.

"Why has my life been so miserable for the past twelve years? Why do I carry a gun and why do I have to sleep with a gun for eight straight years? The only time I am happy is when I am drunk. That's the only way there are no problems. I just drink myself into a stupor. I get to the point where every time I get drunk, I just want to blow somebody's fucking brains out.

"I go into a little introverted world of mine where I don't hear anybody talk to me. I don't know what they are saying. I'm acting like I'm listening but I'm usually thinking about Vietnam, a flashback type of feeling instilled in me because of fear. Like fearful of some guy threatening me. Then I revert back to the old Kill Syndrome that the Marine Corps taught me. You know, 'Kill! Kill! Kill! Kill! Kill!' Sometimes I just dream about that word *kill*."

George began to cry. He spoke of the compassion among the troops in Vietnam, about coming close to death, of men who find their God in war, of his need to be a hero whom other people would respect and admire.

"I've seen a lot of envy," he reflected, "in other people when they know me or observe me, even to the point of revering me."

His father was a much decorated Marine hero, flying over Vietnam before George's tour of duty. George showed me his service record to let me see his citations and decorations: a college graduate, a somewhat All-American guy, state wrestling champion, football star, straight, and no drugs. He saw his sense of fearlessness in Vietnam as a way of gaining his father's respect and admiration. George joined the Marine Corps because it was the patriotic thing to do. He requested guerrilla training and was elated when he received orders to Vietnam.

"I don't think it is hard for you to understand this," he told me, "but now I go so far back to where I would feel the wind, the rain, the fear, the cold sweats, the knotted stomach. Goddamn it, I start crying because of the fear, and because I would shake. Oh, I would cry because I could remember certain incidents." Then he recounted seeing his buddies killed and maimed, torn to pieces, and being gunned down by machine guns, rockets, and artillery shells.

George also told me the details of some gruesome atrocities in which he had been involved, adding, "What bothers me, doc, is I know I did these things in Vietnam. They're always going to be with me, these atrocities. I've never really quite been able to forgive myself for some of the barbaric things I did.

"I deal with my guilt through prayer mostly. Like I sought the Lord's help when I left Vietnam and accepted my Savior.

I've prayed. I haven't talked to the chaplain yet when I'm repentant and can be honest. ... I've lost a lot of faith over the years. ... The point I am trying to make is I'm the kinda guy who's torn between being a good moral person, but my male ego – my masculinity – demands that I present a formidable image to anybody who threatens me.

"I'm torn between the preacher and the killer.

"I had this spiritual counselor at the time of my combat ..., this guiding clairvoyant experience when I'd see what was going to happen. I'd be forewarned – just milliseconds or seconds or up to ten minutes before something happened in combat. This voice would tell me, 'You know what to do!,' and because I followed it and because I did what it said, I'm alive today and talking to you, Harry Wilmer. Yet, at the same time, I've gone through twelve fucking years of mental terror."

Then George told me the first dream:

Trapped

Part I: In the Sewage

I am trapped in water waist deep in a valley in Vietnam. The water is like human waste, like sewage. Full of it. Real sluggish. I find this boat and keep trying to paddle out of the valley. There were mountains on either side of it.

This scene is a picture of the mess he was in over in Vietnam. The human waste had two meanings to me: the wasted people, and the shit and urine that are the discarded end result of nourishment. The problem of the disposal of excrement in Vietnam in the field was primitive. The waste had another meaning to George that I did not know, however. He characterized it as *sluggish* sewage, not exactly the vernacular of the soldier. Why?

The appearance of "this boat" presents a means of getting through the ordeal of being trapped in the valley. The stage is set for a desperate attempt to extricate himself from the mess that Vietnam became for him. In a manner of speaking, the dream shows he is stuck in a deep depression.

The dream continues:

Part II: Not Much Hope

Every time I try to get out of the water by going out of the mouth of the river that flows into it, They [the enemy] are waiting for me, and I turn back. I have a machine gun and shoot a couple of times, and they keep shooting at me.
For the rest of the dream, I keep hiding out in the rocks and going under the water in all this waste. I wake up several times during the dream and then go back to sleep and I get back almost in the same spot in the dream.

These thoughts occurred to me as he told me his dream: He is really stuck in a spot from which he cannot extricate himself. He is trying to escape but is surrounded by rocks, mountains, and enemy shooting at him. The way out via the river that flows into the lake is guarded. He has a boat and a weapon, although they are not adequate to make the break. His efforts to go down into the human waste suggest sinking into the shadow darkness of the unconscious. It may not be to far afield to say that this waste is the residue of "Kill! Kill! Kill! Kill! Kill!"

Since it is my policy first to ask the dreamer for the meaning of his or her dream before venturing my thoughts or associations, I asked George to talk to me about the dream.

He replied: "I am getting out of this boat into what I think is a rice paddy, trying to get out of it. And this was full of shit, and you know how the Vietnamese shit and urinate for fertilization, and all. They do it everywhere. They don't bury it. I've read and I remember pretty much from my college years, and you know Sigmund Freud's interpretations of dreams, and my analysis is that with all this shit in it, and me wading through it, my olfactory sense was very acute. I was in a kind of boat, and there was another man in it, but I don't know if he was in uniform or not. ... "

The dreamer's analysis put more of a Vietnamese color, small, and usefulness to the excrement than I had thought. To my surprise, almost like an afterthought, he introduces another but nondescript man in the boat whom I take to be a civilian part of himself. The man is merely there, however. When I ask George for the Freudian meaning of "shit," he disregards it and says, "I myself decided that this lake full of shit was symbolic of the rice paddies." In other words, it was the cycle of death and creation rather than a dead end for the Vietnamese.

This dialogue followed:

Harry: "Well, it's symbolic of all the shit you have to wade through here before you get yourself on dry land, before you get yourself out of the valley."

George *(cautiously half-agreeing with me)*: "Possibly."

Harry: "And a lot of shit you've got to go through with me."

George: "No. I like you."

Harry: "But you are misunderstanding it. We are going through that stuff because you have to get out of it."

George: "You're helping me dig into my mind. I should not hold back on my language. I just use *shit* instead of *speckled material* or *feces*. In the dream, I have a machine gun I shoot a couple of times."

I saw George twice a week for one hour each time during the six weeks he was in the hospital. He was discharged and a few weeks later readmitted. This time, his ward psychiatrist would not refer George to me to continue our work because he explained to me that it would interfere with the transference to him and to the psychiatric resident on the ward who would be doing psychotherapy with him.

On one occasion when I saw George in the hall, he said to me, "I'm a Dr. Jekyll and Mr. Hyde." We never had a chance to explore his two sides in more depth – Jekyll and Hyde, Preacher and Killer – or the other man in the boat back in the valley in Vietnam. I imagined that this man might be a

Vietnam part of his psyche relating to the fact that on his last day in Vietnam he had been shot and ended up killing the guy who shot him, and previously two marines.

George had said to me at the end of the last session of his previous six-week therapy, "It means so very much to me and to my peace of mind to talk about dreams. I never got to talk to a doc like you at the other hospitals or clinics. This is the most progress I've made in all these years – being with you – and somehow it all came out, and I'm gonna be better when I leave this time. I can't even fit the pieces together again. ... like searching for pieces of bodies. You know, I was lucky to have survived."

He was caught in the moral and mortal problem of worshipping both the Greek god of war, Ares (a ruthless murderer), and the Roman god of war, Mars (a magnificent invincible hero in shining armor).

I never had a chance to try to help him with the pieces again. His treatment would now focus on medication and supportive psychotherapy in the hospital or clinics where therapists don't talk about dreams. I was aware that whether he came to work with me or whether he did not, our professional relationship would create a serious transference problem with the doctors on his ward. It was unfortunate for George that they would not refer him to me again. I could easily understand their position, which implied that they must have regretted referring him to me in the first place. I felt confident that what he and I had learned was not lost, and that is the point I want to make clear to you.

To Master Fear, One Must Learn What Fear Is:

The Fearless Medic in Vietnam

Pete said, "I got bounced around a lot as a child. I didn't have a home for much of my childhood, and forget some people I lived with. My father was an alcoholic, but I don't remember him drinking. When we were living in a mobile home, he said my mother taught me to call him a 'son of a bitch' when he came in. I remember him throwing her out of the trailer and she bounced, and I cried.

"I remember him smashing out a picture window with a broom. I can remember my mother knocking me down a flight of stairs when I was crawling and then, when I hit bottom, spanking me for playing on the stairs. My father was lenient with me usually. I didn't do well in school and dropped out of college.

"Before the war, I was in the peace movement. My feeling was, and still is, I don't know what the hell we were doing in Vietnam. I had friends who died in Vietnam. I didn't understand. I didn't want to be any part of it. It wasn't so much fear with me, but I wanted to have a family and I wanted a 'little me.' I can't see sending nineteen-year-old kids to die for something that doesn't make sense.

"I was going to be drafted so I enlisted to be a medic. I didn't want to go over there just killing people. The guys in Vietnam used to call me Doctor Doom because I had a pretty high body count. You didn't find too many medics that were really combatants. I was. They way they saw it was, I said I was a regular soldier until somebody got wounded. Then I was a medic. So I got into the thick of it like everybody else. I did some strange things. I learned that I could be very violent and could kill people."

Pete told me a recurrent nightmare that troubled him, but unlike most catastrophic war nightmares, the dream did not frighten him as much as the fear of falling asleep and dreaming. It caused him anguish because it touched on the fear of shame in the eyes of his buddies who would see him chicken out and fail to go to the help of a wounded soldier. Pete forced himself, like most combat soldiers do, to act as if he was not afraid – with the expectation that the fearless persona would become a self-fulfilling prophesy.

Cries for Help

Part I: To Cross the Bloody Road

The first thing I feel is heat. It is very hot, and I can smell the pollen from the grass. It's real hot and I hear this guy yelling, "Doc! Doc! Doc!" and I crawl through the grass until I come to the edge of the road. The road is red. He's lying on the other side of the road. I have to get up and go get him. I'm afraid, and that was one of the fears I had – that I would be afraid to go and get my guys.

As soon as Pete had told me that part of the dream, he said, "But that was something that never happened. I always did my job. I never puked out on going to get anybody. They gave me a couple of Bronze Stars for doing that. So I did my job, but in the dream I am afraid."

Pete had implied that he might have been afraid in the dream, but not as a medic in Vietnam. That is to say, he could not admit to being afraid, or that maybe sometime he had hesitated and come too late to help a dying soldier, or even maybe had frozen in his mind if not in reality. His comment that this "was something that never happened," alerted me to the thought that the dream did not repeat a real event. This is an important point because the classical posttraumatic stress nightmare is a repetition of some event that actually did happen and is seen with such unaltered reality as if it were a live replay of a visual record. I have described this phenomenon in my published papers.

Part I is once more like a prologue setting the state for an inevitable next scene, the cry "Doc!" from the wounded man's *scène à faire* to the dangerous crossing.

The dream continues:

Part II: Surreal Ending

Finally [sic] when I get enough guts to cross the road, I get shot a bunch of times. It seems about fifty times, but I don't feel any pain. I just feel the thudding of whatever hit me, and there is blood all over the place but I don't feel any pain. Then when I get to where the guy is at, it's a buddy of mine names Cobb, and he's been dead for a long time. He's one of the first guys I worked on that died. And Cobb just looks up at me and his face is all bloody, and he says, "Welcome home!" and I wake up.

Pete comments, "I thought I was a good medic and most of the guys I got into the chopper were still alive. There were a few times when I couldn't do it. I didn't want to go on this way. When I think about those guys and the mess I've made of my life since I am back home – why did I make it and they didn't? These guys had a lot going for them and I haven't done anything since I am back and I don't understand anymore. That's why I wanted to kill myself. I'm afraid but I don't even know what I am afraid of."

I asked Pete about the strange words from his dead friend ("Welcome home!"), thinking that they were a metaphor for him joining his dead friend in his own death. To my surprise, Pete saw this greeting as his reception when he came home from Vietnam – the big welcome that never happened. Once again, Pete didn't have a home. Everything had changed and he was a forgotten, unwelcome warrior, as he had been a castaway child. He had done everything in his power to create a heroic image, testified to by a couple of Purple Hearts and Bronze Stars. His father and his younger brother were thrilled by his wonderful medals.

He told them about an event on his birthday in Vietnam at a big firefight. The captain in charge was "so petrified that I had to slap him about five times even to get through to what I needed and the guy won a Congressional Medal of Honor. Most guys who got the big medals didn't do anything so brave. They were just there at the right time and somebody saw them. They weren't doing it to defy death. They were doing it because they didn't know any better."

Pete was saying that they were not fearless – they were stupid.

In the dream, there is gunfire, and he is hit repeatedly with no pain but is bleeding. Cobb, "the dead man," is also bleeding, and speaking from another world. Pete had been shot in the leg eight months after coming to Vietnam. He pointed to his right groin and said, "When I came to, I knew where I was, but I couldn't feel any pain. I was afraid to put my hands down to see if my leg was still there. Then when I did feel some pain, I felt my crotch to see if that was still there. But I can remember the seconds that seemed like hours because I was afraid to put my hand down there to see."

Reflections on the Grimms' Fairy Story: "Of the Youth Who Went Forth to Learn What Fear Was"

This is the story of a father who had two sons. The elder was smart and sensible and could do anything, but the younger son was stupid and could neither learn nor understand anything. When people saw him, they said, "There's a fellow who will give his father some trouble!" There are similarities between Pete and the younger brother. In the fairy tale, when the father asked his older son to do something that led him through the churchyard cemetery or some other dismal place, he was afraid and said, "Oh, no, father, I'll not go there. It makes me shudder!"

The younger son heard many people say, "It makes me shudder!" He thought, "It doesn't make me shudder." He asked his older brother and his father to help him learn to shudder. This request led to many terrifying encounters, as well as violent and cruel acts, without him being able to shudder. His fearless behavior appeared more naive and stupid than courageous. Most of the experiences had to do with death, such as spending a night beneath the gallows where seven corpses swung overhead in the cold breeze. So he cut them down and tried to warm them by a fire, but they just lay there and let their clothes burn. In anger, he hung them up again, but he did not learn to shudder.

Another night, men came down the chimney bringing nine dead men's legs and two skulls, and set them up and played ninepins with them. The youth turned the skulls on a lathe until they were round like balls so they would roll better and had a wonderful time playing with them.

One night he was sitting on a bench saying sadly, "If I could but shudder," when six tall men carrying a coffin placed it on the ground by him. The youth said, "Ha, ha, that is certainly my little cousin who died only a few days ago." He beckoned with one finger and cried, "Come little cousin, come" Then he felt the dead man's ice-cold face. He lifted the corpse out of the coffin, sat it by the fire, held him tightly, and rubbed his arms trying to restore his circulation. When this did not work, he said to himself, "When two people lie in bed together, they warm each other," and carried him to the bed, covered him over, and lay down by him. After a short time, the dead man became warm, and began to move. The youth said, "See, little cousin, have I not warmed you?" Suddenly the dead man got up and cried, "Now will I strangle you."

No shudder.

Years later, when he had become a kind and was happily married, his wife became angry hearing him complain, no matter how happy he was, "If I could but shudder ... if I could but shudder. ... "

His wife's waiting maid said, "I will find a cure for him. He will soon learn what it is to shudder." She went out into the stream which flowed through the garden, and had a whole bucketful of gudgeons [small fish used as bait] brought to her. At night, when the young king was sleeping, his wife was to draw the clothes off of him and empty the bucketful of cold water with gudgeons in it over him, so that the little fishes would sprawl about him.

Then he woke up and cried, "Oh, what makes me shudder so? What makes me shudder so, dear wife? Ah! Now I know what it is to shudder."

Vietnam veteran to me: "Look around you. There are still people [like me] out there that are ashamed to say 'I was a

Vietnam veteran' because I am scared that they won't say something to me. I've been insulted, 'Sir, are you one of them butchers over there? Did you enjoy killing them people?' I said 'Hell, yeah, and I'd kill you right now if you want me to. If you don't shut your damn mouth.' "

Harry: "Did that stop them?"

Veteran: "Well, sometimes. Sometimes I had to fight."

More About Vietnam Combat Veterans:

George, A Later Time

"I don't think it is hard for you to understand this, Dr. Wilmer, but I even go so far back to when I would fee the wind, the rain, the fear, the cold sweats, the knotted stomach. Goddamn it. I start crying because of the fear and I would shake [shudder]. Oh, I would cry because I would remember certain incidents."

George was the marine whose story I previously presented under the title "His Thoughts Were Not Evil – His Deeds Were Evil." He returned to see me again to tell me of evil deeds that still lived in his mind. These memories in flashbacks generated such violent and cruel thoughts that one might think the thoughts were evil. They were the reactivation of his marine combat training mentality. At other times, his thoughts were civil and rational.

George said, "I remember seeing a buddy step on a grenade and it blew his leg off, his testicles and everything. Our squad leader stepped on a trip-wire grenade and it blew him to pieces. His arm got blown off. One eye popped out. Half of his forehead was blown away. It was horrifying for me to carry my friend down in my arms. He was shredded to pieces, falling apart and still alive. I don't know if he lived or not. I have flashbacks of killing people, blowing them up or gunning them down with a machine gun."

George had begun by saying that he did not think it would be hard for me to understand about certain incidents of carnage. It occurred to me that these incidents were a prelude to the guilt of catastrophic memories. He was talking to me in the manner of a confession to the father who would understand because he had heard just about everything.

George began to cry as he continued.

"What bothers me, doc, I know these things I did in Vietnam are always going to be with me. These atrocities. I've never really been able to forgive myself for some of the barbaric things I did and participated in. ...

"There are probably hundreds of pictures of me and the other guys in my battalion or supporting company taken of us with dead bodies. We cut a guy's head off once and boiled his skull and painted it fluorescent orange and we got in the bunker in the dark, playing music and moving the jaws like the skull was singing. That one really bothers me."

[Another] "time we were playing baseball with a blown-off leg and a brain. The next morning, we put all the parts in the Amtrak and his brains fell out. Just rolled over. I [had] used his leg for a bat and the other guy was throwing brains at me. I used to play mumbletypeg with dead bodies and I had pictures of me taken with my arms around cadavers, dead soldiers, like we were good buddies. I put cigarettes in their mouths. I did some things like that as a normal healthy man who had been at the top of my class in military school and a champion athlete in high school! That's one thing I'm trying to work on – my guilt. It gets tome when I am around people. I don't like it when I get threatened. I mentally gear myself back into Vietnam and think of all the various ways I'd kill that guy if he provoked me.

"In Vietnam, we called ourselves the 'Delta Death Dealers,' and we carried an ace of spades card. We used to pry open their teeth after we killed them and stick the card inside. Then we'd carry the bodies back to the local village and dump them off.

"You never knew who your goddamn enemy was. It might have been an eighty-year-old VC [Vietcong] or a six- or eight-year-old kid or the regular VC. Once a grenade completely blew this woman away – her skull cap. ... You know how long Vietnamese women's hair was – sometimes four or five feet. I remember doing some lunatic things like putting the skull cap, with a little piece of meat on it with blood stains, on top of my head and the guys that came out of the Amtrak to pick up the bodies [took] pictures of me. I've held in these things for all these years except to other combat marines. They are the only friends I had all these years that I can identify with."

Hellish Nightmares

> **Battle scene:** *I could see blood pouring out of nowhere. I could see the dead faces of friends of mine. I see battles going on and RPG [rocket-propelled grenade] tracers. I hear the explosions of flames and I see napalm going off ... things like that.*
>
> **Prologue:** *I am inside an old house I used to live in but it is back in the Vietnam jungle. I am carrying a gook's head in my hand, just the top of his head, just his eyes and part of his nose. He is dripping blood. I am walking around like I am in a daze. I try to go out the window but the window closes up like the jungle. Then the windows open up and I can see the backyard where I used to live when I was young. I try to clean up the dripping blood, but it's all dirt. I am trying to get rid of the head.*

The dreamer has home and Vietnam mixed up in his mind and is carrying a gook's (Vietcong) head. Being unable to get out of the odd house, he had to find some way to try to get rid of the head inside the house.

The bloody top of the head (remains of Vietnam) cannot be cleaned up. It is dirty. It must be discarded. That seems to be the story line, but what is the plot?

The dream continues:

> *I see this commode and go to it and look down into it, thinking I would throw the head down into it. In the bowl,*

I see a bunch of small maggots on very small dead faceless bodies. I try to flush them down but they start to come back up. I take the gook's head and push it down the commode but [it] starts coming back up, [too,] like when the commode is stopped up. I am trying to push the gook's head down the commode.

I could see the old pecan trees we had when I was a child. I try to get close to the windows, going from one window to another, but each time they returned to the jungle. I wake up.

He was trapped again in Vietnam, as in his previous dream, but now we knew the evil nature of the trap. I asked George to tell me what he thought the dream meant. He replied, "I kinda understand the part about being home. I was going back home but I wasn't all the way there yet, but Vietnam is still in my head. I was in my house and still in the jungle. I don't know what I was doing walking around with that head. I can't get rid of the faceless bodies.

"I still can't get in any dangerous situation, or under bad pressure. I get really uptight, irritable, and can't think or concentrate. I guess one of these days I'll get messed up, stabbed or something, like the guy I shot. I am holding things inside and just can't flush them away. I can't do it yet."

George then told me another nightmare in which he saw ashen-white heads with one eye open and one closed floating around in his head.

"The war is not over really," he said. "We weren't defeated and we didn't lose, so it's not over. I got wounded over there. I can't let it die. I got messed up in the brain, I guess. I can't let it die. It stays in my head."

Nonetheless, he was getting it out – to someone other than a marine, but to someone with whom he could still identify. Recall his powerful attachment to his hero fighter-pilot father who preceded him into Vietnam, and that he was both proud and envious of his father's thirty-six medals. George identified with me as having been a navy captain, but it was more my role as a confessor to whom he revealed his horrible secrets. It was important for him to take time enough to trust me and to know that I would listen to him and not be thinking about myself or psychoanalytic concepts. It was silent listening, just as I had asked him to interpret the dream about the gook's head.

He knew me well enough to be aware that I could shudder, and that I was not afraid to hear his stories or nightmares, and wanted to hear them. To myself, I believed they might give some meaning to his sense of Vietnam's meaninglessness. I was not thinking about a cure, but became genuinely hopeful about him being able to fight the war within.

Notes

1. Friedrich Nietzsche wrote in *Beyond Good and Evil:*

   Man, a complex, lying, artificial and inscrutable animal, weird-looking to other animals not so much because of his power, but rather because of his guile and shrewdness, has invented the clear conscience, so that he might have the sensation, for once, that his psyche is a *simple* thing. All of morality is a continuous courageous forgery, without which an enjoyment of the sight of man's souls would be impossible. From this point of view, the concept of "art" may be much more comprehensive than one commonly believes. (291)

2. C. W. Jung wrote (CW 10):

   *If we wish to come to an understanding about so complex a question as good and evil, we must start with the following proposition: good and evil are in themselves *principles*, and we must bear in mind that a principle exists long before us and far beyond us. (Para. 859)

*When we speak of good and evil we are speaking concretely of something whose deepest qualities are in reality unknown to us. (Para. 860)

*When we pass emphatic judgments we are in an emotional state of mind, and are then least able to apply valid criteria. (Para. 863)

*The reality of good and evil consists in things and situations that happen to you, that are too big for you, where you are always as if facing death. (Para. 871)

*When we observe how people behave when they are faced with a situation that has to be evaluated ethically, we become aware of a strange double effect, suddenly we see both sides. They become aware not only of their moral inferiorities but also, automatically of their good qualities. (Para. 872)

3. In CW: 11, Jung wrote:

If the repressed tendencies, *the shadow* as I call them, were obviously evil, there would be no problem whatever, but the shadow is merely somewhat inferior, primitive, unadapted, and awkward; not wholly bad. It even contains childish or primitive qualities which would in a way vitalize and embellish human existence, but convention forbids. (Para. 134)

Part III
World-Shaking Dreams

The laws of conscience ... rise and proceed from custom, everyman holding in inward veneration the opinions approved and customs received about him.

– Montaigne
Essays I.xxi

Mindless Violence:

Threat of Annihilation

Dream Prologue: Opening Shot

I am conducting a seminar where the students are sitting on the grass in a meadow surrounded by a distant range of high mountains. I am walking around a circle of about ten students, carrying a placard with a calendar of the present month. At the bottom of the page is a black dot by which appear the words: "This is where the comet hit last time it struck Earth."

I stop and tell the students how weird it is that someone has made a mark indicating the spot on a movable sign. Looking at the calendar, I discover that I, too, had made a similar black dot about three inches to the side of the first dot and had written: "This is where the comet will hit this year."

Suddenly I look directly overhead where I see a brilliant white object with a long white burning tail speeding directly down upon me and the group. I brace myself. However, at the last moment the comet changes direction and disappears behind a hill at the edge of the meadow. In the dream, I say, "There was no jolt of the earth, but it was an earth-shaking event."

That is a startling way to introduce a dream. It reminds me that for the past two weeks, I have been following a real comet in the sky, but the dream comet is on a collision course aimed right for me and my students. What should be an earth-shaking disturbance and my death has no impact at all. The comet just disappears over a hill like a spectacular pyrotechnic display.

I wait for the sound of impact or the fiery flash of an explosion which never comes. The prologue suggests that I was expecting something worse than what is happening, and the great danger is already past.

The question naturally is: What happened next? We might hope that it will give me a real or symbolic story of an actual frightening life experience, which I am successfully managing. If it were otherwise, it is likely that there would have been quite an explosion.

The dream continues:

> *I am standing on a long dock at the Pacific Ocean when a grubby man walks out and dumps large crates of garbage into the sea. They have come from the restaurants at the beachfront. I see the garbage sink down in clear water about twenty feet to float around on the black ocean floor.*
> *I walk up to him and say, "You are not allowed to dump garbage in the sea!" He replies in an ugly manner, "Are you going to report me?" I turn slowly and walk away silently, leaving him to wonder.*

On reflection, the moral message may be as clear as the water. In this confrontation between a moral part of me and an immoral part of me, which will dominate? I am outspoken about bad behavior, and lay down the law before I leave him to ponder the punishment.

An archetypal message is that the bad guy (my shadow) reminds me that I must have been dumping my garbage in a public place, trying to get away with it like a Trickster. What might have been a destructive direction was diverted and became a dud.

The end of the dream:

I am at a dinner table seated across from a father whose young son sits at my side. The father relentlessly scolds and criticizes his son in vulgar and hostile language. I listen to his brutal verbal attacks while the son sits forlorn and looking beaten.

I turn to the son and in a firm voice say, "You should do anything you want to do, not what your father wants you to do."

The scene changes and I am alone, in my research laboratory carrying out an experiment that I have wanted to do for a long time.

My father never used abusive hostile language in his endless criticisms of me when I was a child – it just felt that way. The dream father – now a part of me – is, at this moment in time, in dire need of containing his feelings. Comet = urgent news.

Viewed in the perspective of this book, we have a moralistic father (negative superego) encountering a nonmoralizing father. The moral that I derive from the dream story helps the son make a decision – not to obey his tyrannical father, but his other father who will guide him to grow up with an independent mind. His father was dumping his garbage on him, but I am telling the son that he is free to follow and obey his own inner law. To me, the dream was a hit – not spectacular, but memorable.

That may not sound like an earth-shaking conclusion to you, but it was for me. It reminded me that, even at the age of eighty, I have a lot to learn from my dreams about lessons that I knew, have forgotten, or need to be reminded of by powerful new images that tell me stories.

A Nightmare That Changed World History:

"Goodby Dear but Cruel One"

Winston Churchill, a brave and daring man, was fascinated by the British military aircraft early in World War I and began training as a pilot. The predictable life span for that group of pilots was exceedingly brief. His wife Clementine was pregnant and obsessed with the idea that Winston's death would be the end of her child. Her pleas for him to give up flying were ignored.

Then one day she sent him this cable:

> *But after this pleasant day I had a miserable night haunted by hideous dreams, so this morning I am sad and worn out. I dreamed that I had my baby, but the doctor and nurse wouldn't show it to me and hid it away.*
>
> *Finally all my entreaties had been refused and I jumped out of bed and ran all over the house searching for it. At last I found it in a darkened room. It looked all right and I feverishly undressed it and counted its fingers and toes. It seemed quite normal and I ran out of the room with it in my arms.*
>
> *And then in the daylight I saw it was a gaping idiot. And then the worst thing of all happened – I wanted the doctor to kill it – but he was shocked and took it away from me and I was mad too. And then I woke up and went to sleep again and dreamed it a second time. I feel very nervous and unhappy and the little thing has been fluttering all the*

*morning. Your telegram arrived last night after we were in
to announce that you have been killed flying. I had a fright
but went to bed relieved & reassured; but this morning after
the nightmare I looked at it again for consolation & found
to my horror that it was from Sheerness & not from Dover
where I thought you were going first – so you are probably
at it again at this very moment.*

Goodby Dear but Cruel One
Your loving
Clemie

Winston may have talked and reasoned down her pleas and
arguments and discounted her fears up to now, but his
reaction to this letter was instantaneous: "My darling one, I
will fly no more until at any rate you have recovered from your
kitten."

Later he wrote:

*But I must admit that the numerous fatalities of this year
would justify you in complaining if I continued to share the
risks – as I am proud to do – of these good fellows. So I give
it up decidedly for many months & perhaps forever. This is
a gift – so stupidly am I made – which cost me more than
anything which could be bought with money. So I gladly lay
it at your feet, because I know it will rejoice & relieve your
heart....*

Everyone Has a Pearl Harbor:

The Talking Cat

Dangerous experiences in the distant past can surface in current dreams warning us of present danger and giving us ideas of what to do about it. I had the following dream on December 7, 1995, and I did not realize until I wrote it down that this was Pearl Harbor Day. In 1941, I had been in the navy reserve at an army hospital in Panama just before Pearl Harbor.

As I have noted previously, I developed tuberculosis and was shipped home and confined in a sanitarium for eleven months. On December 7, 1941, I awoke after my noon nap, put on my radio earphones, and heard the report of the bombing of Pearl Harbor at the moment it was occurring. Helplessness and wanting to be in the navy during the war added to my utter frustration. I was as powerless as a prisoner of war, tortured by my illness and afraid I might die.

The Japanese struck Pearl Harbor without warning. Our defenses were either inoperable or at sea. At the time of my dream, I had no specific worries and everything was moving along in my life quite successfully. I woke up from the following disturbing dream, saying to myself, "Everything is wrong in this dream about a coming war. What the hell is it all about?" It occurred to me that I was unconscious of some imminent danger just as the commander in the Pacific naval forces had been unconscious.

A Terrible Disaster Is Coming

> **Prologue:** *I am a visitor in a house in Houston, Texas, where I hear that some unspecified powerful world force has declared war on America. Everyone in the house and all the people of Houston are terrified, anticipating great destruction. I am told that the streets and the highways are so crowded that it is almost impossible to travel.*

There is a coming war, an archetypal danger, from which I cannot escape. Houston is the oil, gas, and energy capital of Texas. It is characterized by wealth, poverty, violence, powerful men and women, and institutions. Houston is a typical extroverted big Texas city. The absence of zoning in the city has resulted in haphazard building. The central city is covered with concrete and asphalt so there is flooding during heavy rains. Although there is a generous, brilliant culture in the arts, with kind and philanthropic people and foundations, Houston's images of big money, powerful political figures, and greed are conspicuous.

I am not drawn to Houston, and rarely think of it, so I must be dreaming of it because of some unconscious connection associated with destruction. Given my personal associations, I ask what will happen next.

The dream continues:

Part II: A Talking Kitten and a Contentious Professor

> *I walk outside the Houston house. Midway up the street on the opposite side, I see a tiny kitten on the sidewalk. I stop and hear the kitten speak clearly, saying to me, "I want to find a home." I look closely at him and see that his mouth has a congenital deformity like a hair lip. His body and ears are also deformed. So I ignore his plight and walk on, telling people whom I meet about the wonderful kitten who can talk. I come to an ornery professor who is criticizing everything. He laughs at me when I tell him about the speaking cat. Because of his contemptuous reaction, I turn*

*around and go back to look for the cat so I can bring him
home with me. Unfortunately, the cat has disappeared.*

Who is the cynical, talkative professor whose ridicule awakens me to compassion for the homeless little kitten who can speak up so clearly and poignantly? I had ignored the kitten because of superficial deformities and had bragged about his marvelous ability to talk. A hair lip causes facial disfigurement because of a failure of the two sides of the upper lip to grow together under the nose. This condition can be corrected surgically.

I am put off by the kitten's persona. His plea, "I want to find a home," is ignored in my moral judgment that his need is not worthy of my stopping and responding. The dream says that there is a moment of time in which to do good, and if you fail to act in time there are consequences – in this case, a lost animal and a guilty conscience. The implication is that I must act in time to save myself from the war, and it cannot be done by running away. The dream narrative, having set the stage and formulated the moral decision, must now give us action and plot.

The dream continues:

Part III: Power People and Headlines

*I am in the building where a newspaper is published. The
publisher is being berated by the frantic criticism of the
same professor who laughed at the kitten's plight. He is a
dark intellectual force. The publisher responds to the professor's merciless criticism by saying, "Well, then, you run the
newspaper for a day!" Apparently this happens, because I
am now looking at the next day's front page banner headline:*

*POPE LANDS IN U.S. FOR EMERGENCY MEETING
WITH PRESIDENT*

*After seeing the paper, I want to go home (like the kitten)
and walk outside the building.*

This sequence gives a surreal twist to the dream. He who is a "know-it-all" is given the task to produce his own newspaper for one day. It is a ridiculous story of the power persona of the pope, who has no real power, to meet with the president, who symbolizes the highest United States power. The pope comes for an emergency meeting, implying an urgent need to prevent the coming war. This session is a kind of spiritual politics. One can expect nothing substantial to come of such a symbolic meeting. It is just the morning news.

The dream continues:

Part IV: Stormy Takeover

Once I am outside the newspaper building on my way home, the terrible storm strikes. Black clouds, fierce winds, and a deluge of rain come swiftly. I manage to get in the house where there are other people. With such a storm brewing, we must stay inside the house – where there is a map of the central part of the United States along the Mississippi River. Vast areas of the states are "blocked out" from north to south, including all of Illinois and some neighboring states. These areas are marked as property of the major American oil companies. Oil has been struck in the center of the United States.

The war is represented as an ominous storm, and the map shows that all of the blocked-out areas are the property of large oil companies. The heart of the country is being taken over by big oil, for which Houston is noted. There is no escape for an ordinary individual in a maelstrom where one is helpless. If the dream carries a moral message, it should now deliver the news.

The dream ends:

Epilogue: Let the Old War Heroes Sit Patiently on the Shelf

Finally I walk outside. Suddenly there is no storm. I see a white pickup truck with an open tailgate on which a man is sitting. I walk over to see who he is, and immediately recognize a wrinkled, exhausted, friendly old retired physician – Dr. Russel V. Lee, founder of the Palo Alto (California) Clinic, an energetic, jovial, imaginative, creative entrepreneur who had great faith in me. He gave me my first job as the first psychiatrist at the Palo Alto Medical Clinic in 1949. Lee prided himself on his military career in World War II. He was friends with many great and powerful people.

Sitting next to Dr. Lee is a retired, senile Army colonel whose familiar face shows the ravages of age and old wounds. We are three good friends. I climb onto the tailgate and sit between them. Although I don't feel old in the dream, I get the picture of three old men, like forgotten war heroes … just waiting.

Serious Illness:

The End and Beginning of Everything

My most memorable illness was during the eleven months of 1941 when I was confined to total bed rest in a tuberculosis sanitarium. At age twenty-four, I was a medical intern in Panama where I contracted tuberculosis from a patient dying of the disease on the infectious ward. In those days, TB was called the "Captain of Death." It killed many young doctors. One of my medical school classmates died in the sanitarium while I was there. I had to rely upon the natural healing processes of my body and mind.

Only three years after I left the sanitarium, streptomycin proved to be the first effective antibiotic treatment for tuberculosis. Few human experiences could give a doctor a more powerful understanding of human mortality and vulnerability than a year in imposed, restricted isolation. During the time I was in the hospital, I wrote a successful book entitled *Huber the Tuber: The Lives and Loves of a Tubercle Bacillus*.

After what was called "the cure," I became a research laboratory pathologist studying tuberculosis at Johns Hopkins Hospital. I grew restless because I wanted to treat patients, so I became a fellow in internal medicine at the Mayo Clinic. Within weeks after my arrival, two of my friends on the staff, Robert Hinshaw and Bill Feldman, showed me their research discovery that streptomycin healed tuberculosis in guinea pigs and human beings. By a freak of medical politics,

the Nobel Prize went to the chemist who developed streptomycin, while Feldman and Hinshaw were ignored.

Periods of sickness are predictable life crises. Society provides cultural rites of passage that may help carry us through
all normal life crises. We live these rituals during the day, and
experience them in symbolic form in our dreams at night.
Acute illness has a beginning and an end – recovery, chronic
disability, or death. People are born with some diseases and
we are all born with a genetic predisposition to a variety of
diseases. "Born that way" is our nature from the beginning. A
wonderful Mayo neurologist, Harry Parker, once explained a
congenital neurological disorder by writing in the chart, "a
reference to the biblical words of Jeremiah:

> *Then I went down to the potter's house, and, behold, he*
> *wrought a work on the wheels. And the vessel that he made*
> *of clay was marred in the hand of the potter: so he made it*
> *again another vessel, as seemed good to the potter to make*
> *it. (Jeremiah 18:3-4)*

When I was at Mayo in the late 1950s, I organized psychotherapy groups for rheumatoid arthritis patients hospitalized
at St. Mary's Hospital. That experience is of particular interest
in relation to the dream of the patient I now present.

Crisis: Meaning in Chronic Illness

A woman in her midfifties who suffered from chronic
deforming rheumatoid arthritis as well as pulmonary disease
came to see me because of her depression associated with the
terminal illness of her beloved husband. I shall call her Marie,
a conscientious and skilled hospital administrative worker,
dedicated to patients, to her job, and to hospice patients with
whom she worked on her own time.

After her husband's death, Marie continued to see me,
working through her bereavement. This period was followed
by a heroic reorganization of her life, quitting her secure job

and earning a master's degree in social work at a major university. An acute illness associated with her arthritis required medical or surgical treatment.

Marie was rewarded for her remarkable achievement with an excellent position working on a cancer ward in another hospital. Although I find *empathy* both an overused and a misused word, empathy was one of Marie's sterling qualities. She gave unsparingly of her compassionate self, enduring stresses that took a toll on her strength.

The following dream occurred at a time when she had a pulmonary infection requiring antibiotics, severe fatigue, and a reawakened depression which caused Marie to think, "It would be tragic if, after these years of working and achieving my ambition, I would end so ill that I would have to retire." At the moment of her highest achievement, she experienced an illness crisis. Was all the work, sacrifice, and risk she had taken good or bad? At the time of the dream, Marie had just obtained the antibiotic for her lung infection, and was to see her doctor in two days.

A Wedding Is About to Happen:
Problems for the Bridesmaid

Part I: Selecting a Hymn to Sing

I am the bridesmaid at the wedding of a childhood friend. I don't know what the matron of honor is supposed to do because I have not been able to attend the wedding rehearsal. I ask the bride if she is ready to start the ceremony. She says, "Yes," and asks me to sing a certain hymn, but I don't know the words or the music. I tell her I will sing "Hallelujah." She replies, "I don't want that one!"

The dream scenario begins with a wedding in which the dreamer is to play a central helping role for which she is unprepared. For some unknown reason, Marie had missed rehearsal so she must now make a decision about a hymn. She is on the spot in making a decision that requires the approval of the bride. It is as if she must guess what will please the bride. Instead of her dilemma distressing her because of an ambivalent, indecisive moment, "it felt more like a game to solve a riddle."

A wedding ceremony is a prescribed ritual that provides for some personal and procedural variations. Two people enter a performance area, each with a mandatory final two-word script, "I do," to be pronounced to unify a loving relationship. Its mathematical and symbolic purpose is to make two into one. Its psychological meaning is unity and wholeness. It symbolizes the divine in holy matrimony. Despite the contemporary conscious contempt for some such traditional rituals, the people's unconscious honors them.

Marie's designated role as the bridesmaid is abruptly changed to the matron of honor. That title sounds more like a change from youthful helper of the bride to older honored woman. The absence of the bridegroom in the dream suggests that there are necessary rituals to be found before there can be husband and wife. Marie told me that the specific woman who was the bride in her dream had lived through events that seemed almost identical to her own life experiences.

The dream narrative seems to say that Marie can resolve her present dilemma by identifying the right song – prayer or hymn or spirit. Will the matron of honor find the correct ceremonial music?

The dream continues:

Part II: Solving the Riddle

The bride suggests a hymn, but this time Marie replies, "No! I don't know the words to it." Marie then comes up with the bright thought, "I can sing the Lord's Prayer." The bride is pleased and the wedding will proceed.

I ask Marie to describe the church. She says, "It was a beautiful small old church, all white painted wood with red carpet. The dream was reassuring." The red was the only color in the dream. Red speaks for feelings, passion, fire, and blood,

as well as special honor. I asked Marie for her association to
the red.

"It is vivid like [the word] *fear*, which sounds a little like
fire," she replied.

I thought, but did not tell her, my association that the
dream *fear/fire* might relate to her real-life *fever* – Marie's high
temperature that led her to call her doctor for an antibiotic. To
have countered her association with mine seemed like carrying an interesting thing too far, like a game. Better leave it
with her idea.

Marie smiled with pleasure as he told me that the Lord's
Prayer "is said at mass and is the model for all prayers":

> *Our Father, who art in heaven, Hallowed be Thy name. Thy*
> *kingdom come. Thy will be done on earth as it is in heaven.*
> *Give us this day our daily bread. And forgive us our*
> *trespasses, as we forgive those who trespass against us. And*
> *lead us not into temptation, but deliver us from evil: For*
> *Thine is the kingdom, and the power, and the glory, for ever.*
> *Amen.*

This is how our dialogue proceeded:

Wilmer: "What is your association with the dream church?"

Marie: "Reminds me of a church to which I was recently
invited to attend a healing ceremony where I heard a woman
channel healer who spoke about how she had instantly healed
a sunburned woman in a healing ceremony like this one."

Wilmer: "*This one?*"

Marie: "*That* one. It reminded me of a time when I burned
my finger badly and went to the emergency room. The nurse
looked at my finger and kept me waiting two hours to see a
doctor. The pain was severe, so I decided to meditate all the
time that I waited. Suddenly I was aware that the pain had
gone. When the doctor came in, I told him that I had meditated ad the pain had gone away. He replied, 'Oh, no. This has
to hurt.' He gave me some pain medicine, and another medi-

cine. I didn't take any of the pills. My burn healed up without any blister. It just dried up."

Wilmer: "What does that remind you of?"

Marie: "Last Friday when I called my doctor and had to speak to his nurse, I told her that I was in urgent need of some antibiotics. She said she would tell the doctor. I went to the pharmacy but they had not called in a prescription Friday or Saturday. I wouldn't be able to call them until Monday, so I meditated and invited my own healing powers. I got the medicine on Monday. I had the dream that night."

Wilmer: "What does the dream say to you?"

Marie: [Silence. No reply.]

Wilmer: "Have faith."

Marie: "Yes! And when I feel I am floundering like now, just let things be. Let up. When I am not feeling up to par, and am functioning at less than par (or at least not optimally), and I begin thinking of myself as incompetent, just let things go. Meditate or pray." [Pause]

Wilmer: "Your unconscious – the dream – is seeing you in a positive way. It is giving you a role in assisting a new life beginning, a youthful image of the woman who is exactly your age."

[I wait. Marie remains silent.]

Wilmer: "There are no men in the dream, so it is a dream of your feminine self, not deformed or incapacitated but proceeding through ritual, a rite of passage. It shows you that it is not yet time to sing 'Hallelujah!' but the Lord's Prayer is the right decision."

Death:

Dreams of Psychotic Patients

I conducted dream seminars for schizophrenic patients on my ward at the VA hospital. Most analysts are not interested in working with the dreams of psychotic patients. My psychiatric colleagues were indifferent. The VA chief of psychiatry let it be known in a disapproving way that working with schizophrenic dreams was not in accord with VA policy. Medication was in. Psychotherapy was out. Antipsychotic medication can mask the voices and images of schizophrenic hallucinations and delusions. The world of the psychotic is a different reality. It is very real to the patient, but not to the therapists who are relieved to have medication to blot out the crazy stuff. I used medication in modest amounts plus dream analysis.

To examine moral conflicts and judgments in dreams – the dream-data of psychotic patients – was of value to me and my patients. That is a moral decision: The value of studying their dreams is better than not studying them. Their dreams presented more vivid images of the struggle between good and evil, light and dark, heaven and hell, than the dreams of ordinary people. Once the psyche's deepest gates are open, primitive, scary, and strange forces emerge.

Such dreams may appear as parables and high drama. The nature of the conventional (Freudian) unconscious reflects events in our personal real-life stories. The collective (Jungian) unconscious, however, is beyond personal elements of our outer lives. Its images, symbols, and stories reveal the existence of a common humanity of all human beings. Often both unconscious elements appear in the same dream. Call them archaic, if you wish, but they exist in all of us. It is no wonder that the public stigmatizes the mentally ill and casts them aside. The problem, however, is that all the crazy things in the psychotic world exist in the lower basement of everyone's psyche.

Dreams of schizophrenic individuals give us a data sample of moral purpose, or force. The boundary between normal consciousness and unconsciousness is invaded by the deeper unconscious. The dream is raw natural human data whose existence is not to be ignored.

A schizophrenic patient whom I will call Henry told the following dream to me and the dream group:

> *I am a three-year-old child sitting on the lap of an old man who is radiating in a bluish-white light that shines on him from above. The most striking thing is that he is glowing himself. I know that the light was familiar to the old man but it was an overpowering unexpected experience for me. Nothing is said or done but I am overwhelmed by the total experience. Looking closer at the man, I discover a glowing small red area on his neck.*

That was the dream.

It was fascinating how attentive and quiet the entire group of psychotic patients was. I was equally intrigued by the quiet, dramatic way Henry told the dream. I imagined a glorious old man, almost godlike, with a dangerous red mark on his neck. I asked Henry what he thought was the message of the dream. He replied, "Something had happened and would not go away." These words came across to me as a powerful metaphor.

What does one do or think about a significant event that will not go away, and hounds the mind? I asked the members of the group to tell him what meaning they could make of his dream. One of the patients was particularly intrigued by the lights and colors in the dream. The bluish-white light came from above as if from heaven, and the red light on his neck was an unexpected finding. Another patient asked Henry what had happened in his life when he was three years old.

Henry told us that this was a recurrent dream he had had ever since he was three years old when his grandfather had died of cancer of the throat. He thought the cancer had been at the same place as the red glowing mark. Another patient asked Henry when he spoke of radiating light, did that mean his grandfather had had radiation therapy?

First things first. We talked about his grandfather's death as clearly as Henry could remember it. The catharsis in a caring group of psychotic patients created warm connections contrary to the stereotype of the disconnected withdrawn schizophrenic. The ritual process of the group made them whole for a little while.

In concluding the group, I told Henry that it seemed as if he could not let the memory of his grandfather die, suggesting that he had grieved all these years, and was still grieving now for the loss of his grandfather. Is unfinished grief not a terrible thing for all of us? Time does not heal everything. This recurrent dream of a trauma I call the "healing nightmare."

From an analytical point of view, Henry's dream expressed both his personal, unconscious, repressed life experiences as a small child, and the nonpersonal, collective unconscious.

Why talk about the collective unconscious? Because therein lies a special meaning in our common humanity. What had gone away was a grandfather figure holding Henry in a loving connection. That is what happened and would not go away. Viewed from a collective perspective, the grandfather's periodic return in the dream is a reminder of a loving, comforting father figure, and at the same time a warning light indicating the need to let him die. It was as if Henry's grandfather would not have peace and rest until he could safely slip away into that other world of death. As an archetypal dream of death, its meaning is transcendental. An artist might suggest that the light rays from heaven indicated the direction of an ultimate journey. I would be remiss not to suggest an association of a redeeming God and a hell on earth (being killed by cancer eating one's throat where we eat). The Catholic church believed that dreams were messages sent by God – *somnia a Dei missa.*

The moral decision that I take from the dream is that Henry ought to accept the past as dead, because otherwise it will not leave him alone. Something had happened that wouldn't go away. He must take the next step so that which had happened would then be dead history. It might help him come back to life.

Notes

1. John Bunyan begins *The Pilgrim's Progress*:

> As I walked through the wilderness of this world, I lighted on a certain place where was a den, and I laid me down in that place to sleep, and as I slept I dreamed a dream. I dreamed, and behold I saw a man clothed with rags, ... standing in a certain place, with his face from his own house, a book in his hand, and a great burden on his back. ... I looked, and saw him open the book, and read therein; and as he read he wept and trembled, and not being able longer to contain, he brake out with a lamentable cry, saying "What shall I do?"

From a point of view of morals and dreams, it is worth remembering that John Bunyan had joined the Baptist church in England and refused to bow to royal edicts banning nonconformist preaching. This action led to his imprisonment from 1660 to 1672. For those twelve years, he read the Bible and Foxe's *Book of Martyrs*, and wrote many books. In 1675, he was again imprisoned, during which time he wrote his most celebrated work, *The Pilgrim's Progress*.

2. One of my patients had this dream two days before her mother's death at home:

> I am with my mother, who is dying in bed at home. She asks to see her brother Henry. I say, "Mother. Henry is dead. You have to remember he is dead." I go out the door which leads me into a very large room with a high ceiling but no discernible features or furnishings. It is a large space. I hear a voice call me from above. I look up at a large window and see Uncle Henry standing there. He says, "Here I am. Tell sister I'm here and I'm happy and everything is okay." I race back to mother and when I get there she is gone. I wake up and sit bolt upright in bed – certain that my mother has died at that instant.

3. C. G. Jung writes in CW 10:

> In view of the fact that dreams lead astray as much as they ex-hort, it seems doubtful whether what appears to be a judgment of conscience should be evaluated as such – in other words, whether we should attribute to the unconscious a function which appears moral to us. Obviously we can understand dreams in a moral sense without at the same time assuming that the unconscious, too, connects them with any moral tendency. It seems, rather, that it pronounces moral judgments with the same objectivity with which it produces immoral fantasies. This paradox, or inner contradictoriness of conscience, has long been known to investigators of this question: besides the "right" kind of conscience there is a "wrong" one, which exaggerates, per-verts, and twists evil into good and good into evil just as our own scruples do; and it does so with the same compulsiveness and with the same emotional consequences as the "right" kind of conscience. Were it not for this paradox the question of con-science would present no problem; we could then rely wholly on its decisions so far as morality is concerned. But since there is great and justified uncertainty in this regard, it needs unusual courage or – what amounts to the same thing – unshakable faith for a person to follow the dictates of his own conscience. As a rule one obeys only up to a certain point, which is determined in advance by the moral code. This is where those dreaded conflicts of duty begin. Generally they are answered according to the pre-cepts of the moral code, but only in a few cases are they decided by an individual act of judgment. For as soon as the moral code ceases to act as a support, conscience easily succumbs to a fit of weakness. (Para. 835)

Part IV
Control of The Mind

Sanity is madness put to good use.
– George Santayana
Little Essays

Impulse, Anger, and Blame:

A Stern Steady Hand

A very attractive young woman whom I will call Susan lived at the mercy of her impulsive decisions which led to a series of woefully miserable relationships with men. She could see at the end of each relationship how blind she had been. Nonetheless, Susan would still cling to the fantasy that *he* would have been the right man if only *she* had behaved differently. Still proclaiming her love, she was unable to see that it might have worked out if *he* had behaved differently. Thus, she was at the mercy of her fantasies and could not stop acting them out. So she would end up with another similar man. The cycle went on until she began to withdraw from any intimacy as if she were cursed. Susan became depressed.

The depression led her to blame men, all men, as the source of all women's relationship problems. Her feelings associated with this extreme generalization kept her from any commitment to any man, and it was a hostile signal to any man to beware. Some men rose to the challenge. Her depression served a purpose in slowing her down, turning her mind to introspection, and bringing forth a series of fantastically interesting dreams and a wish to find out what they were telling her.

The details of her life story that led to her attitude and behavior need not be recounted here. Susan came to me because I was a Jungian analyst who was especially interested in dreams, and had helped some of her friends. She had

written an emotional letter to her recently discarded boy-
friend and he had not responded.

She told me this dream:

Letters, Gorillas, and Orangutans

> **Prologue:** *I am trying to mail a letter to someone in a
> foreign country, but the letter is returned to me by a man
> who says, "There is no way to get the letter through." I am
> utterly frustrated because it seems to me that this letter is a
> matter of life itself, like a warning. I feel that if this is not
> received, something terrible will happen.*

We are given this preliminary information which spells out
the essence of the dream motif: a life (and death) letter that
cannot reach the person to whom it is addressed. That scene
sets the stage for the ensuing story. Certain questions are
planted in our minds: Who is the man Susan is trying to warn?
Why is he unreachable by the ordinary mail service? What
must she get through? Who is the man who returns the letter
to her? If the letter is so vital, is there another way to convey
the message? What is the terrible thing she wants to forestall?

The dream continues:

> *I know that the letter can be delivered. I don't understand
> why it is returned to me. It is addressed to someone who is
> doing field research on gorillas or orangutans in Mexico, in
> the Yucatan [peninsula in the south].*

The addressee is identified as investigating, in wildlife, two
jungle primates of different species which live in different
parts of the world.

The gorilla lives on the ground in the lowlands of equatorial
Africa, and is the largest species of ape. Male gorillas weigh
about 450 pounds and have an arm spread of nine feet. The
dominant male (silverback) usually leads a harem of two to
fifteen of the much smaller female gorillas.

The word *orangutan* means "forest person" in Malay because the face of the young orangutan looks human. It lives in the swampy coastal forests of Borneo and Sumatra. The males are sexually aggressive. The orangutan is an arboreal animal, living in the trees swinging from branch to branch with great dexterity.

This second sequence establishes a remote jungle setting where there would be highly problematic mail service. The assurance of being able to deliver the letter suggests a sense of confidence about getting the message through. Is this a warning message of life? Is the terrible thing *death*?

The dream continues:

> *A station wagon appears with a family of five Mexicans. They seem illiterate. They have vacant faces, but I know they are happily enjoying an outing and are indifferent to anything else. I speak to them in English about the letter, but they don't understand. They speak only Spanish.*

The dreamer does not speak the language of the people who might know the answer to her question. The picture of a happy Mexican family together on an outing is the image of people who are

expressive of their emotions and have strong family and generational bonds. Mexican males pride themselves on a macho image and are demanding of their women, as if they are possessions. What can Susan learn from such a different culture?

The patient – highly intelligent and financially secure, but sad and depressed – is shown a glimpse of ordinary, poor, illiterate people who have the happiness and family ties that she would like but cannot find. In contrast to Susan's heavy preoccupation with what other people think, the Mexicans are sufficient to themselves, seeking pleasure in relationships and focused entirely on their outing.

The dream continues:

> *Then an attractive young Caucasian woman gets out of the
> station wagon. She is wearing a white jacket with pastel
> stripes on it, just like I have. She is self-assured and walks
> confidently. She says, "There is a way to get that letter
> delivered. Don't worry. Give it to me and I will see that it
> gets there." I give her the letter.*

Dramatic event! Out of the Mexican family station wagon
comes a vibrant, confident image of herself to whom Susan
gives the letter to be delivered. The message of gorillas or
orangutans relates to primitive masculine aggression and
domination. From this inference, I suggest that the subject of
her investigation (analysis of depression and the collective
unconscious) was the masculine power part of herself that
had been operating in a wild way. A new version of herself
suggests a hopeful outcome.

The dream continues:

> *I go into my room in my house where I find two men
> shooting rifles at objects like straw hats, pictures, and
> things hanging on the walls. The men have been ransacking
> my things. Al the drawers are pulled out and their contents
> scattered around. I am not frightened but angry. When I
> appear, they stop shooting. I think they are afraid that I will
> press charges. I say, "Okay, just get out of here." They leave.
> I wake up.*

This is the denouement. Susan confronts her destructive
dark side and stops its wild behavior. One message could be to
learn from the happy family outing of people who readily
express emotions of relatedness. The dream research uncov-
ers her own destructive masculine gunmen who have opened
all her drawers and are shooting carelessly but not dangerously in her own room in her house. From a series of uncertain events, the dreamer finally makes a stern, unequivocal
moral judgment: "You must stop. You must get out of my life.

You must go". This scene also suggests her sexual life and previous relations with men that brought her to see me.

Susan finally faces her inner torment without fear, but with feeling – with anger – to get the shadow men out of her life. She also reveals her potential power: the threat of pressing charges to bring her negative side to trial and punishment – a threat of a moral judgment.

Getting the Message

Prologue: In a Fog

I am driving along a country road in a beautiful pastoral scene in England. Suddenly a fog rolls in and surrounds me. I have a special pair of glasses that have a correction so that I can see through the fog.

I'll call the dreamer Julie. She is on a journey in a beautiful place when suddenly she is surrounded by fog. Apparently there is an unexpected obscurity interfering with her vision about where she is and where she is going. *Mirable dictu* ("wonderful to relate"), she has some glasses with a correction that cuts through the opaque fog. This development suggests that she has the capacity for unusual insight to clarify her journey in the inner landscape of her mind. The question is, "Where is she going?"

The dream continues:

I drive on until I come to a parking lot, where I get out of the car and walk straight ahead toward a shopping mall. But between me and the mall I see a hill, or you could say a "small mountain." I ascend the hill along a winding, zig-zag road to the top and then descend the other side until I come to a large wooden lodge like a log cabin. It is the shopping center. I enter the front door of the lodge. The room is empty.

The road seems to dead end in a parking lot near the shopping mall. The dreamer's journey has gone from a pastoral nature to a parking place, from which she must go on by foot. Julie is immediately confronted with another obstacle, not a phantom-like cloud riding the wind but a substantial heap of earth. She starts unhesitatingly to surmount the mountain straight on, not trying to get around it. This act approximates a moral decision in her unconscious. In accord with Jung's theory of compensation, her dream takes a position that positively compensates for indecisiveness in conscious life.

Julie has no difficulty climbing to the top of the hill and down the other side, where she expects to find an ordinary shopping center. Upon reaching her destination, however, she does not find a collective, commercial enterprise but rather a solitary wooden lodge. She walks in the front door. There is no hint of danger.

This segment of the dream suggests that what she is seeking lies inside this rustic, simple lodge. But what is it?

The dream concludes:

> *The lodge is empty. There are an upper floor and a basement. I go down to the basement where I am surprised to find a post office. A postmistress behind the counter asks if she can help me.*

The end is not a resolution of a conflict or tension, and the problem presented by the dream is how to make her way to a post office in a basement of a remote log cabin. I assume that Julie has come to a post office in the unconscious (basement) where a helpful woman handles all the messages coming and going. This post office is not a destination, but a final stop from which items will be delivered to the addressee.

Julie is the destination or, to put it another way, it is her destiny to be there when the message arrives. Perhaps the message she has not yet gotten is that she is quite capable and able to proceed with her own independent journey despite her fears and doubts. It is as if the dream itself says, "Look, I have examined your strength and determination, and I see nothing to fear on that score."

Take Note of Proverbial Words:

The Surface Is Deep

When dreams are short stories, they may be allegorical or proverbial truths that influence the dreamer. From a dramatic point of view, this case is often condensed in a powerful punch line. The life of the dreamer is less important than the moral of the dream. Take, for example, the following dream in its entirety:

> *I have planted an extensive garden. It is like the Garden of Eden. It is much nicer than any garden I have ever planted in real life. I have neglected my garden for a while and there are children playing in it. Although I am angry at them, I know they need to play so I don't punish them. There are rows or mounds where I planted the seeds, with furrows or channel between them.*
> *I call out, "Play, but not where the seeds are planted!"*

That dream does not need interpretation. While it is a woman's dream, we can imagine it as a man's dream. Each way would have different implications that would be evident to the dreamer on reflection. The moral decision is to play in nature, following the rules of the game, and the outcome will be fruitful.

For Those Who Talk Too Much:

A Brief Clear Message

Somerset Maugham once wrote a short story entitled "Mr. Know It All," about a man who not only knew everything but also talked relentlessly and listened to no one. He had an explanation for everything. People detested him, but he had ruled out any value to what other people thought, felt, or had to say. We all know variations of Mr./Mrs. (or Ms.) "Know It All." Unfortunately, under pressure, most of us can become the know-it-all, especially when it comes to explanations.

In my practice, I have worked with many people whose outstanding difficulty with their children is when their off-spring misbehave or are rebellious. At such times, when the parents take a stand of authority, they feel a need to explain everything – to talk it out. This compulsion, I believe, is a carryover from the psychology of the need to talk every conflict over. It follows a previous authoritarian childrearing culture where obedience was demanded, children were ordered to obey, and parental authority was not to be questioned. This approach characterized the patriarchal customs. I have poor results in telling my patients to make their stands and say what they want, but they do not have to explain everything.

We also know people who talk all the time, in unpunctuated speech, leaving no space for the listener to interject his or her reaction or opinion. This listener is not only frustrated and overwhelmed but sometimes falls into a silent, sullen, rejected state. When this conduct is extreme, the talker is euphoric as the listener sinks into angry depressed space.

A group of individuals who commonly talk too much includes therapists, counselors, psychiatrists, and analysts. Many analysts regularly scold themselves when they realize that they are talking too much. Parents, teachers, and people in authority who talk too much may be defending themselves from listening to lesser people whom they believe have no right to defiance. Naturally, this approach breeds conscious and unconscious rebelliousness. Talking becomes a matter of power and control of the airways, not communication.

I began this section with a moral judgment that there are people who talk too much. Am I right [*sic*] in judging what is too much? My answer is important in the context of this book. Yes, I am right in judging when someone else is talking too much. I am a member of a professional guild of psychiatry, psychology, and psychoanalysis, which espouses a common belief that its members ought not judge or blame. The accepted belief of analysts seems to be that the unconscious is not moral, and is probably amoral. This principle helps them from interjecting their own biases in their interpretation.

This assumed neutrality, however, is most often a bland pretense of being masters of their unconscious countertransferences.

In the beginning, the psychoanalyst sat in a chair behind a patient who, reclining on a couch, regressed to some early childhood state. Having deliberately created and defined this situation, can the psychoanalyst ever take a "value-free" or neutral position after already defining its value? The analyst creates and expects a certain verbal and physical behavior, and any nonconformity would need to be analyzed as pathological resistance. Fortunately, there are few remaining rigid, classical psychoanalysts.

It was always easy for me – on the couch – to figure out the feelings, biases, and power problems of my analyst in spite of his carefully modulated speech whenever he did talk. To continue to play out the analysis, one has to accept the sham of this neutrality. The analyst may say very little, be totally unresponsive, or silent for long periods while requiring the analysand to talk frequently.

"Keep free associating" or "What are you thinking?" my Freudian analyst would say when I became silent for any length of time. The very basis of the "talking cure" was talking it out with a master of the art and craft.

Being Captain of Your Ship:

Ending Hassle in the Crew

One of my dreams occurred while I was attending a national meeting of psychoanalysts held at an elite hotel on San Diego Bay near the naval station. Warships glided through the water outside my window, stirring old feelings from when I was in the navy.

At that time, I was troubled by a conflict in a professional relationship. It felt like a miniwar inside me. I had been blamed for a statement that was exactly the opposite of what I had said. No explanation clarified the misrepresentation. It was as if there were two truths. Conventional wisdom would be to talk it over, to reason and try to reconcile the differences. If two people can do that, anger and misunderstanding disappear, but if that cannot be done, anger persists, confrontation occurs, and reason is a casualty.

The basic problem is power and who is in charge. Would my dream give me a clue as to a moral decision in a hassle where each party believes he is right and the other is wrong? What ought I to do?

The answer may be in a dream I had during that time:

> *I am seated by my old friend, Sir Laurens van der Post, at a banquet table in a luxurious hotel. I am surprised that he is there because (even in the dream) I knew that he had recently died at the age of ninety. He says that he has come to give a lecture "at the run-down Brown Hotel." In the*

dream, I knew that the Brown Hotel was one of the finest old hotels in London where famous and wealthy people stay. Sitting at the table with me and van der Post (a biographer of C. G. Jung) there are two young women candidates to be Jungian analysts. They know me, but I cannot remember their names. They play silent roles.

I ask van der Post for a copy of his latest curriculum vitae because I am going to make a documentary film of him in which he would talk on "Jung and Hope." I also tell him that I am writing a paper on the same subject myself. Van der Post asks me, "What is the title of your paper?" I make up a title on the spot: "On Not Talking It Out." As soon as those words are out of my mouth, I am struck with the realization that this is a brilliant idea. I think, "I should take that message to heart."

Van der Post then asks me to give him an example of not talking it out. I say that when you are telling a child to do something, and the child becomes argumentative, ornery, and resistant, don't talk it out. Don't explain your decision. Just give your opinion without any explanation and then there is no argument from opposite points of view. It is like the advice of the old judge to his young replacement: Give your opinion – it will probably be right – but not your explanation. It will probably be wrong.

I say, "Take the case of a navy captain who is given an order to launch a ship. He does what he is told. He doesn't ask why."

In the dream, I become the navy captain who is seen launching a small gray patrol torpedo boat into a bay off the ocean. It is wartime. I know that the two destroyers normally patrolling this harbor looking for enemy submarines have gone out to sea, leaving the harbor undefended.

I tell a little girl standing on the beach that there is a war going on and that she will have to go back home and wait because her father is the civil defense fire warden who has to put out any fires started by enemy shells.

The moment I awoke, I knew the dream was talking to me about the tense encounter I had been experiencing with an analytic colleague. In the dream, this was dramatized as a war where the homeland was threatened by a large submarine that lurked in the bay. A submarine in such a dream can be said to represent a deep sea monster or dragon, and I set out on a heroic mission to kill the sea monster in the water of the unconscious.

Sir Laurens van der Post appears in the dream because he was on my mind. Just before he died, he had sent me his last book, *The Admiral's Baby*. Van der Post lived a courageous, adventuresome, and spiritual life. He undertook many diplomatic and discovery missions for the British government. On more than one occasion, he came to the defense of oppressed and despised minorities, and is said to have single-handedly saved the African bush people from murderous extinction. Yet his real significance, towering reputation, and worldwide affection and admiration did not come from his heroic life, but instead from his compassion, integrity, decency, and amazing ability as a storyteller in his books.

I served as a captain in the U.S. Navy Medical Reserve Corps during the Korean War. That and my hard work with Vietnam War casualties and Jung brought van der Post and me into a close friendship. He had been planning to come to Texas to visit with me, and my last letter about that visit arrived in London a day after his death. It seemed to me that he had come back to be with me in a distinguished setting to see that I learned my lesson "on not talking it out."

That was the moral decision in the dream, as if it said, "Thou shalt not resort to useless talk, but give yourself clear, brief, unequivocal directions. For example, 'Do your duty,' an elemental moral edit of military life." I associated this nautical dream adventure with the small whaling boat launched to kill Moby Dick. That image would suggest the mythology in humankind's insatiable drive to win against the overwhelming power of nature.

In the dream, I tell the little girl what is happening and send her home where her father was a civil defense warden. The child represented civilian life and the feminine nature of humanity – earth, hearth, and home – and the promise of the growing child.

After I accepted the strong message of the dream, my tension (war) subsided. Once more I was at peace after assuming my own autonomy. There was tranquillity where there had been explosive feelings and dread.

The problems of appreciating the idea of not talking it out are many. The talkative extravert may never really see the wisdom in not talking it out. A withdrawn introvert may not even have considered talking it out, and "not talking it out" is superfluous advice. Most people are between the extremes of extraversion and introversion. There is a good chance they will understand the wisdom of this idea. The older they are and the more rigid in their patterns, however, the less likely that this idea will even register in their psyches.

This idea is therefore addressed to the youthful folk of any age, and those who are able to suspend their habitual attitudes and beliefs. They can understand and even use this idea in real life and find its wisdom. It is the verbose talkative people, whether barely literate or brilliantly intellectual, who are at the mercy of their own seductive talk.

The point of this kind of specific admonition is that only when it occurs in your own dreams, and you listen to it, does it really matter. Other people's dreams do not count for much in our own lives.

Transference: Projection on the Dream Analyst

– Good Analyst/Bad Analyst

The dream may contain a figure that is obviously the image of the real therapist. When this is the case, we may assume that the dream figure personifies attitudes, thoughts, or feelings that the dreamer harbors about that person. This concept can be either astonishing news to the patient or confirming information. The dream figure may be affirming, frightening, or depreciating, giving insight to both the dreamer and the analyst. Their relationship may be erotic, loving, dreadful, hating, or dangerous. It is a projection, hooking onto both reality and fantasy. The power of the transference dream explains why the therapist's explanations and interpretations arouse feelings far beyond their words and ideas. They are highly charged.

When a dream is perceived as a guide to moral and ethical decisions, the question naturally follows, "Is the moral enigma that of the dreamer or a projection of the analyst?" It is precisely this point that leads many people to the conviction that dreams have no moral purpose except that which the analyst reads into them. Yet even when the inner doctor is identical with the outer doctor, it is still necessary to ask whom he or she really is.

For example, a high-achieving woman, plagued by doubts and fears of failure, became despondent. Her work and success were in jeopardy. She felt trapped and sinking. Her gloom cast her husband and ten-year-old daughter in darkness and helplessness. She came to me for therapy because of her rich dream life and because I was a Jungian analyst. I'll call her Shirley. She related this dream:

> *My daughter and I are in the cockpit of a rocketship that is just taking off. I am immediately aware of the oxygen masks and tubes hanging down around our necks. It seems as though I am in a commercial airplane and realize that the pilot has not told the passengers to put the masks on their faces. I am extremely scared and wonder what has gone wrong and what is going to happen to us.*
>
> *As the rocket ascends, I find that I cannot breathe. I know that I am not dead yet. I ask if Dr. Wilmer is the pilot.*

Some life-threatening malfunction has occurred as the rocket lifts off. The oxygen apparatus automatically drops down as in a commercial jet. Shirley cannot breathe and feels that she is dying. The pilot has announced no instructions to the passengers. Is he negligent, dying, or dead? Am I the pilot? All we know is that Shirley is asking that question, and the dream does not say that I am the pilot. We can assume that the instructions are well known to her. Why doesn't the mother put on her mask and then her child's mask, and start breathing oxygen before she and her daughter become unconscious and die of suffocation?

The rocket indicates traveling at a great speed. That notion calls for patience to wait for her spirits to lift her up from morbid depression, inertia, and lethargy. The moral paralysis seems to suggest: To be or not to be, that is the question. To survive, you must take care of yourself immediately. Do not wait for an authority figure to tell you what to do. You are your own pilot in life.

Warning: You must not become too dependent on your doctor. That is bad for your future. You must take care of your child so that both your older self and your younger self can survive together.

Dependence on the Father Figure

A fifty-year-old physician came to me for help. Let's name him Walt. His spectacular success in the practice of medicine and accumulation of beautiful material possessions took all of his energy and he had never taken time for peaceful tranquillity or to look at his inner or spiritual life. His wife had died suddenly of a heart attack a month before he had called me for an appointment. Walt was choking with grief and feelings of guilt for not having devoted more time to being with his wife. He was tormented by "if only" thoughts that might have saved her. His minister had urged him to consult with me.

Walt had experienced a bad relationship with his father who ignored him or, instead of listening to his son, would lecture to him, scold him, and judge whatever he did as wrong. Father knew best. Father was the final authority on everything. That approach had psychologically crippled his son so that Walt often could not act independently on his own behalf. My patient maintained close ties with powerful senior physicians. He told me about his present situation and some of his life story before he related the following dream, which he had had the night before his first appointment:

> *I am brought into an emergency room suffering from a great gash wound that laid open my left chest. I know that looking into it, one would see my lung and heart. There is no bleeding and no pain. This injury is just something that had happened to me. I guess you could say that, despite the magnitude of the trauma, I don't have any feelings. I lie on*

the operating table in the ER. No doctor or nurse comes to examine my wound. I see you, Dr. Wilmer, on the far side of the ER just standing there and looking at me without any expression or reaction. I am mad because you are not concerned about me and will not do anything. I woke up frightened and angry with you, and remember that I have this appointment today.

The following dialogue occurred next:

Walt: "I was angry because you were the doctor in charge of the emergency room and were ignoring me. In that kind of emergency, you are supposed to do something immediately. You didn't even come over to look into my wound. There were other doctors in the room. I just lay there with my big open wound. 'Do something – don't just stand there!,' I thought. A doctor is trained to do things. I was frightened because I thought I had chosen a doctor who was not going to help me, who wouldn't say anything."

Wilmer: "Do you feel you made a mistake now that you are here with me?"

Walt: "No, but in the dream, *no* doctor on the emergency room staff would even examine me."

Wilmer: "*You* are a doctor!"

Walt (after a long silence that spelled total surprise to me): "That is right!"

Wilmer: "You weren't looking inside. That's what we are going to do here. The physician side of me was trained always to do something. The psychologist side of me was trained to listen and help you see things that you are not seeing, or at this time can't see."

Walt: "Oh. I get it."

In this man's dream, I was in the room with him and there was no doubt that it was me, although when he had the dream he had not yet seen me. It was his clear picture of me, so I was named.

This dream told Walt that his problem was very deep, that it had torn him open, and that he was numb from the shock. The fact that the big wound was not bleeding meant that this was a symbolic wound. The dream did not mean that he was going to have a heart attack, but rather showed us his identification with his wife. Walt was not yet ready to look at this aspect, but that was an emergency anyway. Without any specific interpretation, I knew he understood that his work, so to speak, was laid out for him to heal himself in the right place. I made a mental note to watch for the appearance in dreams or associations of himself a symbol of the archetype of the Wounded Healer.

Transference: A Case of Mistaken Identity

When analysts see themselves personified in patients' dreams even though the images are obviously not theirs but those performing a function resembling that of an analyst, the analyst often announces some variation of, "That's me." If it is a powerful, positive role, he or she seems anxious to take credit, and if it is a negative role seems anxious to be that important. It is my rule of thumb that when this image is not clearly identifiable as me, I think of it as the patient's inner analyst or guide.

I remember consulting a famous classical Freudian psycho-analyst in Chicago in 1957 when I contemplated a move from the Mayo Clinic to Palo Alto, California. I sought him out because I felt I had lost my way. Our sessions we e not formal analysis with me on the couch but instead sophisticated conversations in which he urged me in the strongest manner to move back to California and rejoin the San Francisco Freudian scene. I was in anguish because being on the staff of the Mayo Clinic fulfilled my highest ambition in medicine.

At times of crisis in my life, I have usually written a children's book around a fantasy. This time, I wrote and illustrated a book I titled "Everybody Is a Nobody Sometime," about a little boy named Arky who was lost in the Land of the Nobodies which also went by the name of the Land of Asif. There Arky found that he was an actual nobody. Nobodies had heads, arms, and lower bodies but no upper bodies. Arky was befriended by the King of the Nobodies and met a little girl Nobody, Gloria Goodenough. They fell in love.

The King, Gloria, and Arky set off from the Wantmoors of Asif with the help of Crusader Sir Pecevere Right-Rite, a knight in full armor who carried a large sword. The Crusader led them up a very high mountain to the Castle of General Ernest Lee Becoming, the Wise Old Man who told them how to get home via the Land of Asis. Crusader led them all to the final destination, where they all immediately were transformed into Somebodies. In the end, Arky (as he was running) fell over Stumble Rock but picked himself up, brushed himself off, and announced, "I really am somebody, and it wasn't much of a fall at all."

The story came to me in a week. Its meaning was crystal clear to me. Both at my beloved Mayo Clinic where I had trained and in the presence of the famous psychoanalyst, I felt like a nobody although I knew perfectly well that I would not have been invited back to join the staff at the end of my tour of duty in the navy if I were not already somebody.

To remedy my lost feeling, I imagined a journey in search of reality from Asif to Asis. On this fantastic trip, I was joined by a loving young girl and my father figure, the King of the Nobodies. We set off on an arduous climb up a steep mountain led by a figure who suddenly appeared. I assumed that he was my strong masculine military personality who was blazing new trails, Crusader Sir Pecevere Right-Rite. I identified the crusader's uniform and sword with my navy captain's gold-braided visor and white uniform, and my navy dress (ceremonial-rite) sword that I brought from Washington to Rochester. The general at the mountaintop I associated with the wise old man, and the picture that I drew of him bore a striking resemblance to C. G. Jung.

One day I brought the text and the pen and ink drawings to show to my famous analyst. Before I could say a word about the story or the pictures, he excitedly jabbed his first finger at Sir Percevere Right-Rite and exclaimed, "That's me!"

"The hell it is. It's me!," I said to myself.

I silently nodded, however, and sadly put my children's book away. I have always thought that the false Sir Percevere had led me astray.

When I try to explain to students how the projection of the therapist onto a figure like him or herself is more than likely a case of mistaken identity, I tell them the following story: When one is in a crowded room and sees a familiar face across the room, one might walk up to that person and say, "Hi, Roger!" only to realize that although there was a resemblance, it was not Roger at all.

My patients are invariably grateful and happy when I tell them that the figure whom we had wondered if it were me was actually their own inner guide and analyst. When I am not around, that guide is with them – not me.

In the Face of Danger:

Your Dream May Paint a Reassuring Picture,

So You Can Make the Right Decision

A man consulted me because of panic. While certain medications will diminish panic, silent listening is the first step. Giving medication is the doctor doing something, taking action. The first question I ask myself is, "Can the patient do it himself or herself?"

Just working with a psychiatrist you can trust and respect, whose presence creates an atmosphere of confidence, is powerful medicine. A physician my decide against giving an active drug, and prescribe a placebo ("please"), an inert substance that often has a significant psychological effect. The very presence of a silent, listening, empathic physician who does nothing can also have a placebo effect.

My panic patient was a competent, successful businessman faced with a horrendous decision. Divided by feelings of both obligation and adventure, he was unable to decide. He was not distraught by compulsive ambivalence but rather by fear that something terrible was going to happen. After he had seen me several times, he reported a dream:

I am standing near the base of a high dam, and I'm terrified that it is going to break. Suddenly I hear a strange crushing noise. I get into my car and speed down the riverbed. It is rough going and I rush to get out before the water comes cascading down. I am astonished to see you sitting in a camp chair in the riverbed as if there were no danger. I drive on wondering why you are so calm. I wake up reassured and don't feel any panic.

The dream does not need interpretation. It is its own reality. The therapist could make symbolic or Freudian interpretations but what would be the purpose, except to please the therapist. The dream had its effect. Why try to outdo nature's artistry? This is transference, too.

The Devil Made Me Do It:

Encounter with the Trickster

Schizophrenic patients related dreams to a patient group seminar that I conducted once a week on my ward. Psychotic patients generally see right through sham and pretense. In this way, they are like small children before being taught in school and society to accept sham as if it were true.

Many years ago, I saw one of my psychotic patients confined in a continuously flowing, warm, sedative tub of water singing a sailor's chantey. I asked him the name of his ship. He shot back, "Can't you see? I'm in a tub, you boob." My sham was offensive. His was a parody on the truth to deny any power satisfaction that the attendants might have had in imposing this treatment while acting in the caring role. I have never since tried joking about a patient's difficult plight.

It is a common excuse to say, "The devil made me do it," or to ask, "Where the devil is it?" as if the devil had hidden it. Schizophrenics often see and talk with the devil. When doctors face a delusional patient, they are apt to think, "Yes, I know you think it is the devil, but it really isn't. It's a fiction of your mind." A delusion is seeing something that is not there, but to the patient demons are there as real as the doctor is. I ask such patients to tell me about their devils.

C. G. Jung spoke of the reality of the psyche, and postulated that the inner world was, psychologically, just as real as the outer world. He even went so far as to say that the concept of the reality of the psyche was one of his most important contributions. Delusions occur in the waking conscious patient even though they are living in the unconscious being. Most analysts I know do not want to work with dreams of schizophrenic patients.

A patient we'll call Edward tells the following dream:

To Look or Not to Look:
That Is the Question

Prologue: *I am at a party where everyone is in costume and wearing a mask. Then a man appears out of nowhere, wearing a Joker costume. He looks just like the picture on a playing card. He walks up to me and tells me to follow him. We walk off.*

The setting is a cheerful masquerade party at which no one appears as he or she naturally is. The celebrating people are disguised in costumes. The prologue presents the archetype of the persona. The intent of the Joker – Trickster or devil – is to lead Edward away. Where will they go? Who will be there? And will we ever get to identify the party people? Is this opening scene a metaphorical image of the patient's psychiatric ward? Does the encounter with the Trickster represent a discovery of a hidden part of Edward?

The dream continues:

I now find myself in another room where there are a whole bunch of Jokers in the same kind of costumes. As we enter the room, everyone pauses and cheers this Joker with me. As he walks through the little group, everybody is bowing to him. I remain in the back of the room by the door. He walks up onto a stage at the front of the room. Everyone becomes quiet and sits down. The main Joker starts talking on stage. I can't make out what he is saying but the tone of his voice is very low, very slow, very seductive. It is unforgettable.

*Everyone just stares at him, like everybody's hypnotized by
him. You know, they just stare with their mouths open,
looking amazed at what he is saying.*

Here is action without words, the power of one personality
in the midst of a group of people with similar personalities –
jokers. All attention is directed to the principal joker and his
words. Everyone is under his power. He has followers. We
have moved to a position of power and authority in the guise
of a Trickster.

Edward hangs behind near the door, holding himself at a
distance and in a spot where he can escape. It is safe to assume
that some important conflict is being told in words the
dreamer cannot hear. The questions to ponder before we
proceed to the next sequence are: How will the hidden issues
be revealed or uncovered, and into what form will the Trickster transform himself – that is, what are his tricks?

*I am not looking at the Joker but at the crowd. I just listen
to the tone of his voice, when all of a sudden ... something
like ... I don't know ... I just turned around and turned my
back to him like somebody had turned me around. I kept
listening to the tone of his voice and was about to turn
around to look a his face when I heard another voice
pleading, "Don't turn! Don't turn! Don't look at him. Don't
turn."*

*Fear comes over me. A man's voice keeps telling me, "Don't
turn! Don't turn!" I am tempted to look at his face because
his voice is seductive – very low, very flat. I have never heard
one like that. I am struggling between the two voices.*

*I wake up. My heart is beating really hard, and I'm perspir-
ing. I get up and look around the room and realize it is just
a dream, but for a minute it is so real that I can't figure out
for myself, when out of the dream, whether it is real or just
a dream. I get up and read the Bible for a while.*

The moral indecision in the dream is whether to turn around and look at the Trickster or not. One possibility is that the trick of the Trickster was to split half of himself into an unseen, unknown, and seductive presence with a different and contrary voice. If this is a split in two, was this a split personality? He became invisible in front and a disembodied voice behind. The struggles were both psychological (symbolic images) and physical (racing heart, perspiration, fear). According to this line of teleological reasoning, once Edward had resolved the moral issue of which way to look, he would be able to make a clear distinction between the two worlds of "only a dream" and waking consciousness in the morning.

I told Edward that both voices were probably his voices – that he was both demon and the redeemer. There was a big struggle inside him as to which of many roles to play, as in the opening party ("Guess who I am!") and in the end: whether to separate and follow the shadow's seduction, or walk on and turn his back to his Trickster.

In 1901, Jung began to try to understand the meaning of the bizarre mental life of schizophrenics, and often found an amazing parallel between the patients' delusions and mythological motifs. At that time, Jung (himself a physician) noted that the clinical approach to the human mind was only medical and mostly concerned with the anatomy of the brain and not the human mind, "which was almost as helpful as the approach of a mineralogist to Chartres Cathedral."

Schizophrenic patients are thought to live in a dream world, because their unconscious and the dreams invade consciousness. As Jung wrote:

> *The mere fact that they have such ideas isolate[s] them from their fellow men and exposes them to an irresistible panic, which often marks the outbreak of the manifest psychosis. If, on the other hand, they meet with adequate understanding from their physician[s], they do not fall into a panic, because they are still understood by a human being, and preserved from the disastrous shock of complete isolation.*

Notes

1. A poignant, tragic, but inspiring child's poem of acceptance was written by an unknown child in a Nazi death camp. It was given to me by Father Oliver Johnson of Austin, Texas, who found it in a book of Jewish poetry:

> From tomorrow on I shall be sad.
> From tomorrow on,
> Not today. Today I shall be glad,
> And every day, no matter how bitter it may be,
> I shall say:
> From tomorrow on I shall be sad,
> Not today.

2. I had the good fortune to attend the extraordinary 1961 symposium "Control of the Mind" (the proceedings of which were compiled into a book edited by Farber and Wilson) at the University of California, where Aldous Huxley said:

> In passing from this field of improving the intelligence and the awareness, from these techniques for realizing and for implementing the old command "Know thyself," let me quickly point out that it is a curious and distressing fact, particularly in our civilization, that we are apt to propound very high ideals and to issue deep moral injunctions without ever offering the means to implement the ideals or obey the injunctions. We have been saying "Know thyself" for an enormously long time, but we never have put forth, as did the Sanskrit people, 112 exercises for knowing thyself. So often we find in our particular civilization this curious assumption that exhortations and commands will of themselves help you to obey these exhortations and implement your good intentions. In fact, however, they don't, and you have to propose at the same time means by which to fulfill them. (p. 71)

3. I ask myself, should you or should you not accept the present, and where you are in place and being what you are? The answer will depend on how you interpret the word *accept*. If it means passively taking whatever, then you might as well wallow in a pig sty or a prison or a position of degradation and not stand up for yourself. In my lexicon, that would be bad. You will have to accept where you were born and when you were born and the time you were born. You may deny them, but they are immutable facts.

Sages have written that if we will accept things as they are and what has happened, rather than wishing they were different or could have been different, we would be content and at peace. One of the cardinal rules in human relationship is the need to accept the other person as he or she is. Once you do that, you can make a good decision. Acceptance of the present is a way of saying "yes" to life.

4. A few rules on how to control your mind at moments of critical decision:

I. Accept the given situation and calm your emotions so as to see if despite your doubts about *what is*, it might be the better of the possible alternatives.

II. Accept *what is* so that you may either change it or yourself to find a healthy way to live with it.

III. Do not accept *what is* but stay. Stand your ground and speak your mind straight without malice or anger.

IV. Do not accept *what is*, and when you have mastered your anger and your wish for retaliation and revenge, find somewhere else that *can be*.

5. The danger is that if you do not follow the rules to control your mind, you will likely fall into the Land of the If-onlys and What-ifs, where the quicksand sucks you down and you lose your footing. In following these rules, make Charles Darwin's words from *The Descent of Man* your motto: "The highest possible stage in moral culture is when we recognize that we ought to control our thoughts."

6. C. A. Meier, writing on the dramatic structure of the dream, notes one of Jung's recommendations:

which has proved of great value in actual practice, and that is to understand the dream as a "drame intérieur." The structure and course of the dream would then be similar to the structure of drama, drama in its ancient traditional form. We recall that Schopenhauer calls every dreamer a Shakespeare and makes him the "Theatre Director" of his dreams. That is where the romantic view that the dream is the origin of poetry and drama has its place. Although Jung published these first findings in 1945, he had been making use of them for more than twenty years.

Let us assume that the structure of classical drama is something like this:

1. Indication of place, time and dramatis personae.

2. Exposition (*desis*), initial situation, involvement, weaving of the plot.

3. Peritpetia (*krisis* = decision) or culminations, dramatic climax, crucial events, presentation of transformation (possible catastrophe).

4. Solution (*lysis*), meaningful conclusion, result.

Let us now go through a dream divided up by Jung in this way in the work mentioned above:

1. I am in a simple house with a farmer's wife.

2. I tell her about a long journey to Leipzig.

3. On the horizon there appears a monstrous crab, which is also a saurian and which sort of gets me in its claws.

4. Miraculously, I have in my hand a divining rod and I touch the head of the monster with it. It collapses and dies.

To avoid giving the impression that this is just a coincidence, let us take another example from Jung:

1. I am on a street corner. It is an avenue.

2. In the distance a car appears, approaching rapidly. It is being driven rather unsteadily and I think that the driver must be drunk.

3. Suddenly, I am in the car and apparently I myself am this drunken driver. But I am not drunk, just oddly insecure and as if I have no steering-wheel. I cannot control the fast-moving car and crash into a wall.

4. I see that the front part of the car is smashed. It is a strange car that I do not know. I myself am unhurt. I think with some uneasiness of my responsibility.

For our third example let us look at how the initial dream of a depressed patient fits into this schema.

1. I was fishing for trout, not in an ordinary river or lake but in a reservoir, which was divided up into various compartments.

2. I was using ordinary fishing tackle (flies, etc.). I was having no luck.

3. As I was growing angry and impatient, I picked up a trident that was lying there.

4. And immediately caught a splendid fish.

It is obvious that there will be dreams that don't fit into this schema. Personally, however, I must confess that since getting the idea from Jung I have come across remarkably few exceptions. ... In private practice and in many seminars the method has proved itself hundreds of times. ...

If the dream brings a solution to the conflict, this would in terms of ancient drama, sometimes appear as a *deux ex machina*. ... In connection with the dramatic structure of the dream, we cannot avoid the "Poetics" of Aristotle, from which, with Jung, we have already borrowed the schema for the structure of the drama.

7. Primo Levi, in his book *The Drowned and the Saved* (a dark meditation on the Nazi extermination policies and his experience in Auschwitz), wrote:

> The best way to defend oneself against the invasion of burdensome memories is to impede their entry, to extend a *cordon sanitraire*. It is easier to deny entry to a memory than to free oneself from it after it has been recorded. This, in substance, was the purpose of many of the artifices thought up by the Nazi commanders in order to protect the consciences of those assigned to do the dirty work and to ensure their services, disagreeable even for the most hardened cutthroats. The *Einsatzcommandos*, who behind the front lines in Russia machine-gunned civilians beside common graves which the victims themselves had been forced to dig, were given all the liquor they wanted so that the massacre would be blurred by drunkenness. The well-known euphemisms ("final solution," "special treatment," the very term *Einsatzcommando*, literally, "prompt-employment unit," disguises a frightful reality) were not only used to deceive the victims and prevent defensive reactions on their part: they were also meant, within the limits of the possible, to prevent public opinion, and those sections of the army not directly involved, from finding out what was happening in all the territories occupied by the Third Reich.

Part V
Good

"Tut, tut, child!" said the Duchess.
"Everything's got a moral, if only you can
find it."

– Lewis Carroll
Alice's Adventures in Wonderland

A Conversation Called Analysis:

You're a Bad Girl, and Don't Ever Forget It!

Patient: "I keep scolding myself saying that I am bad, impossible, can't do anything of significance. I begin things but can't complete them. I know I will mess them up. I've felt that way since childhood. No amount of worldly success stops this feeling of terrible self-judgment. I am convinced that I will fail in any task I dream up."

Wilmer: "You told me last time that you felt time was running out, that as you were getting older you might just as well give up trying and stick with volunteer work and social life, because you will never do anything great."

Patient: "Right. I feel guilty all the time."

Wilmer: "No wonder. You're always calling yourself 'bad.'"

Patient: "I had a dream last night:"

I don't have much time to get to a party. I am rushing around trying to find the right clothes. When I am ready to go, I get into my car and speed off, but another car blocks my way. It is small and silly looking, like a clown laughing at me. So I get out and go into a bakery nearby. Its window and cabinets are filled with luscious desserts, pastries, cakes, and elegant delicacies. There is a cake sitting on a counter that is already sliced and part of it gone. I take a little piece of cake and icing in my hand to eat it. I feel guilty and look to see if the clerk or store owner sees me. She is nowhere in sight, so I continue nibbling on it like a child.

Then the owner comes out and sees me. She smiles and cuts off a piece of cake and gives it to me. I am embarrassed at first, but then happy.

Wilmer: "What do you think that dream means?"

Patient: "That I did not really deserve the cake, and then being treated like a good little girl. It was just given to me on a silver platter – the story of my life."

Wilmer: "But it is not the story of your life that you have been telling me. You've been telling me that you were always bad, and never got the prize you wanted."

Patient: "Yes. Wasn't I?"

Wilmer: "No, you weren't being bad. You were being naughty."

Patient: (Silent, nodding)

Wilmer: "You have a party to go to, a social celebration, but in the beginning you were not in good shape so far as appearances, but you could change that and get going."

Patient: "But the silly car blocked my way."

Wilmer: "Not a bad message! You are in too much of a rush, as if you don't have enough time. That is your story. The car was an obstruction forcing you to stop [*sic*] taking everything and yourself so seriously. A little humor, please. Enjoy yourself more. Lighten up, as if you are in a good mother's kitchen."

Patient: "I like that."

Wilmer: "More importantly, the dream shows you – a moral judgment – that you are not bad, but naughty. It is a dream test that you passed. Not only did you pass, but you got the most important gift of all, acceptance for whom you are. The store owner is the psychological good mother inside you, who by the way has found her role and succeeded in it. She was happy and forgiving."

Patient: "She was. I like your idea of calling my being 'bad' as being 'naughty.' "

Wilmer: "You don't have to take my word for it. That is your dream."

Patient: (Silent, nodding)

A Warning: Short, Sweet, and to the Point

*A **Dream of Mine:** I am suddenly aware of a sharp pain in my right leg. I examine it and find a small tack stuck in my right thigh. I pull it out and wake up amused.*

Association: A bureaucratic administrator at the VA had ignored or rejected a series of suggestions I had made to improve the psychiatric service. I was still angry with his arrogant attitude when I had fallen asleep. The dream problem was all mine. What was it trying to tell me?

Interpretation: When I woke up, I said to myself that the trouble was a little tack. With a little "tack," I said to myself, you could remove a thorn in your side. That struck me as so funny that suddenly life seemed tolerable and my pain was gone. The unconscious has a punning sense of humor.

After the Nobel Prize, What Then?:

Through the Toll Booth

I invited two Nobel laureates in chemistry to the Institute for the Humanities at Salado recently. I spent the weekend with them, moderating their seminars and lectures. The speakers were Paul Berg and Michael Brown, both impressive, inspiring, and quite open. The two men were modest yet brilliant, each with a delightful sense of humor. They spoke in friendly conversation with the audience.

I also gave my first lecture at the institute. It was on "The Quest for Silence," and received a standing ovation at the beginning and again at the end. This experience was my high point since I founded the institute seventeen years ago. I have now turned over its direction to my successor, and spend my new free time writing books and plays in my greenhouse. This transition involved coming down from high public visibility and giving up control as president, a suitable idea since I was in good health and the institute was flourishing.

We have had ten male and female Nobel laureates as speakers. My identification is not with them but with the pleasure of success instead. The following dream occurred after the last lecture at which I was in charge. It sent me a message about retirement and another path to a place of creative life:

Prologue: Last Word from the Antarctic

I am in touch with a scientific station in the Antarctic. It is in a small square room directly under the South Pole. I receive a report from the station saying that they are reaching absolute zero. At that temperature, all life at the Antarctic station will end. Rather than reacting in horror, I see this occurrence as the ultimate scientific achievement.

A more astonishing image of an apparently impossible achievement could hardly be imagined. I reluctantly say that it is a cold-blooded view of theoretical physics. It is, however, the end of a long, isolated, cold, and dedicated labor. I am "in touch" with these events, not a part of them.

The prologue says that in my unconscious there is a buried frozen laboratory at the very end of the earth where death and extinction of life approach. As a prologue to a drama, I cannot imagine any sequence. The scientists will not get the Nobel Prize.

My personal association with the Antarctic began when I was in the Navy and was a member of the Antarctic Task Force of Operation Deepfreeze to select people to spend a year in the Antarctic. This stage was part of the First International Scientific Antarctic Research Program. I wanted to go to the Antarctic, but for many reasons did not apply.

Yet I had always wanted to visit this region. It is a coincidence that in July 1997, when I relinquished the leadership of the Salado Institute, my wife Jane and I went on a trip to Spitsbergen, a Norwegian island in the Arctic Ocean about seven hundred miles from the North Pole. We were in the planning stage of this travel as I had the above dream. The Arctic was somewhere in my mind when I fell asleep.

The dream continues:

Part II: Great Heights

I am looking across a deep valley in Switzerland at an Alp where at five thousand feet I see a twisting road which was built by one man. I am bewildered that it is only five or six feet wide. This is a famous valley and the mountain range is so high it looks more like the Himalayas than the Swiss Alps.

Again I am getting my perspective from a distance, seeing a remarkable path built by one man. The road is deserted. The vision is spectacular. It reminds me of the town of Murren in the Lauterbrunnen Valley of southern Switzerland where Jane and I visit every year, looking across at the Jungfrau, Mönch, and Eiger. The road suggests one man's high but narrow, deserted achievement. It is a remarkable symbolic path he had constructed by manual labor.

This part of the dream looks to me to be a dramatization of the institute not in the sense of grandiosity, but rather as the result of hard physical and mental (achievement) labor. I love the Swiss Alps and have vacationed there every year for the past twenty-six years, up to 1997 when it was the mountains, fjords, ice, and animals of Spitsbergen – exploring a new space.

The dream continues:

Part III: The Toll Booth on an Ordinary Freeway

It is morning and I get into my new car to drive off to work in a big city like Dallas. I come to a toll booth that stretches over an eight-lane highway. A young inconspicuous man is seated in the car next to me. I am distressed because my car won't accelerate and only goes at a dangerously slow speed while cars are speeding by and cutting in and out.

I think the problem is that I don't have any gas, but I realize that I do have gas. I stop. The young man and I get out of the car, and together push the car across the lanes to a gas station located by the toll booth. This was a very dangerous maneuver because of all the speeding cars, but we had to get off the road to the gas station. It seems miraculous that we escaped without being hit.

The end of the dream brings me down to earth in the dangerous traffic of a big city, the opposite of the Arctic and the Antarctic, and a road where there are no peaks. The problem of the car that won't accelerate and finally stops and must be pushed suggests that I should slow down and get out of the fast lane. I need to get to the side of the road – on the sideline, not the big dangerous "playing field." The toll booth has two associations to me: Dallas, and the pun on the word *toll* that this journey has taken on me. A toll booth is also a threshold or passageway to another road where you have to pay the price, but I do not get through the toll booth and am stuck on this side. Fortunately there is a gas station, a sign that I can get help.

I have the feeling that the gas station (which I never see) might represent my greenhouse where I get my energy to go on with my own personal creative work. The presence of the young man helper in the dream means that my younger side still exists and can give me a push if I get stuck. In my forthcoming book *Silence*, I speak of ultimate silence as "absolute zero," a place we never reach. In the dream, I am not able to pass through the toll gate, but I have not come to the end of the road. I did not get a Nobel Prize, but a Salado artist made a bronze bust of me which will appear in Bill Moyers's narrated film on the Salado Institute.

I really prefer the small things and the quiet things in life. At eighty, you should not go 80.

Being the Good Mother:

Moral Counsel in Word and Image

A woman we'll call Ellen relates a dream to me:

> *A conscientious, caring mother is standing in her garden where she has planted two turnips. It is her intention to leave them alone to compete with their roots. In the dream, she thinks they represent her two daughters.*
> *A very old man from centuries past comes up to me. He strikes me as a brave, wise, casual, and quiet man. He speaks in the Arabian language. I say to him, "What does this mean?"*

The dream begins, like a prologue with a mother placing her "daughters" in rich garden soil to let them grow, relate, and struggle without mother's intervention. Suddenly a man, like an archetypal image of the Wise Old Man, comes from the near East speaking Arabic. Ellen asks him a profound, existential question.

The dream continues:

> *The scene changes and I feel that what I see is his (symbolic) answer to my question. I see flower stems growing through a rock, realizing that they had to struggle hard to bore through it. The flowers overcame the resistance of the rock. (Their pale yellow blossoms resemble the yellow turnip flower with the purple color of the plant.)*

I am now inside my house, where I see one of my books sliding over the edge of a bookshelf. Part of it is hanging down and I know it is about to fall to the floor. I reach up and push it back from the edge, rescuing it from falling.

Words are hopelessly inadequate to answer Ellen's question. A vision of flower stems bursting through solid rock appears. The Old Man's image tells her that the feminine stem and flower grow with great power and determination. In a sense, one could say that the soft feminine power is irresistible to the hard obstructing rock that she associates with the masculine. The flowers or her daughters find their place in the sun.

This is the story of the outcome of Ellen's mothering of her daughters, but I assume that the daughters, being offspring of the mother, also represent the youthful aspects of the mother and show her new growth. I naturally wondered what the dream was saying about Ellen's personal life story and the knowledge and wisdom she was gaining in her analysis. Will there be a final message, or a closing image like an epilogue?

The dream continues with a new episode:

I am on the street searching for my car, but cannot find it. I search a long time and finally accept the idea that it is lost. Without my car, I cannot get around. I am stuck. Suddenly a bright idea dawns on me: I must go back and retrace my steps from the way I came into this place and then I might find my car.

I start to do this and see two triangles in bright colors. They have rays or streamers flowing from their right sides that look like scores on a page of music. This scene is so beautiful and marvelous that I think it should be hanging in the Metropolitan Museum of Art.

The dream says that Ellen must go on searching and that to do so she must go back and retrace her steps to find her own unique pattern of individuation. I compare her search to that of a detective who, when baffled, retraces the steps of the person being sought. That pursuit is very much like retracing one's life story in an analysis.

The moral imperative of the dream is explicit when it says what the dreamer must do. It is not equivocal, or "you figure it out," but instead clear succinct orders. They are not specific in telling the dreamer exactly what to do but rather how to go about it, or what attitude to take.

Unloving Money

People often say, "Money is the root of all evil." They have got it all wrong. The Bible says "the *love* of money of the root of all evil." Money is not evil. Moral and ethical decisions constantly involve money. Without getting into a long discourse about money, gold, and greed, or the necessity of having money or its equivalent to survive in any society, I suggest that money represents both soul and shadow. No one I have ever known has had enough. My richest patients lived in fear of losing what they had, and ending up penniless.

The dream world can help a person find values that transcend objective wealth. It is too visionary to preach that we should transfer our love of money to symbolic and abstract ideas or words. I stop my discussion at this point in deference to Charles Darwin's statement in *The Origin of Species*, "We will now discuss in a little more detail the struggle for existence."

A wealthy patient was flying high, acquiring new businesses, and creating mergers. I will call him Bert. He had consulted me because of mood swings and phobias. He was elated and inflated, and as he said, "making money head over heels." Bert compared his obsession with money to the artistic drive of Georges Seurat, who was totally absorbed in making paintings and completely lacked relationships. Bert loved the 1996 Pulitzer prize-winning play, "Sunday in the Park with George," which wove the story of the artist around a single painting. Moreover, the financial success of the play was icing on the cake. Mostly Bert liked icing. The extravert Bert's comment on the play was an enthusiastic, "Good show!"

Bert wore a big Texas Stetson hat and boots. In fairness, his image was a genial, handsome, strong, taciturn, and rich Texas trying to acquire a large European corporation. The following dream perplexed him, thus making him angry. He announced to me that he didn't like the dream. I asked him, "Why do you have to like it? Maybe *that* is the point." He looked at me with a smidgen of contempt.

The dream begins:

Prologue:

I am driving my new car to the airport to catch an overseas flight, but I don't know where I am going. I have lost my airplane ticket, but that doesn't stop me from rushing to catch the plane. It is thirty minutes to takeoff time, but I am more than an hour from the airport. I step on the gas.

Bert is alone, frustrated, and speeding. The prologue makes a clear opening statement: He cannot possibly make his flight unless there is some extraordinary event. The nature of Bert's frustrating race made me wonder how he will manage the impossible situation into which he has gotten himself. Will it end in simple failure or will it have a surprise symbolic ending? Bert sees himself as a fast-moving entrepreneur, doing the show all by himself. "I don't know where I am going." With a lost ticket, this statement could have at least two meanings: his commercial European destination, and where he is going in life. Giving himself a short time to get to the airport means he is not preparing himself for his venture.

My interpretation is that while being shown a story of his life, Bert is taught a moral lesson: It is bad (wrong) to go so fast for an elusive goal that common sense would tell him was impossible.

The dream continues:

I am dejected, standing by the side of the road. I realize that I have forgotten my briefcase, so that even if I had made the plane I would not have my necessary papers and passport with me. I will have to turn around and go home again. Just as I reach to open the car door, a bird falls from the air and I think its neck is broken. I pick it up and hold it in my hand. It is crippled but it flies off into the sky.

Bert agreed that the dream was showing him to be in too much of a rush and he had to slow down and simplify his life. I suggested that he cannot make the timetable he has set for himself, and he has left his identity and passport behind. Some analysts would say that this interpretation indicates his therapy but since there is not a single aspect of the manifest dream, that suggests me or his analysis. I think it simply says that he must turn himself around or his bird spirit will crash. It, too, must stop flying for a while but, the story says, can take off again even though it is crippled. Maybe Bert does have to get his life together in a more artistic way, and not in a materialistic way.

Family Values:

When Being Bad May Be Good

Politicians advocate "family values" as if the concept were an obvious good thing. "Family values" range from noble ideals to murderous values of the Mafia family, and the appeal of the words *family values* rests in their simplistic use as a hallowed invocation to heal seemingly insoluble problems. There is little doubt that the values of children reflect the values of their parents, and can be inculcated in the children's children. Few people would disagree that children generally behave as their parents and parental surrogates *do*, and not as they *say*. Display of family wealth is very important to the children's need to be special and appear better than other children. That is the meaning of the words *"Lord it over. ... "*

Money is of no interest to babies, whose blissful happiness is priceless. Babies live a time of love and joy, except in the presence of negative family values such as abuse or being unwanted, rejected, and despised. Philosophers discuss, define, and argue about the good, the bad, virtue, and evil. Ordinary people know what is good and what is bad without explaining, and readily pronounce, "That is a good (or bad) dream," or "That is a good (or bad) decision."

Now to tell you about a patient I call Rita. She was a good child, obedient, respectful of her parents and teachers, and hardly ever got into trouble. She was indulged. From the point of view of social and psychological growth, it would have been better if she were less good and sometimes bad. She knew how to have a tantrum but not how to rebel. Rita was the oldest of three daughters of wealthy parents who lived in "the big house on the corner." From what I have said so far, you will have surmised correctly that her parents were socially prominent, and very proud of their Rita. They liked to show her off because tat reflected so well on them as parents. Sometimes Rita was blue and downhearted but never knew why. She was told that she had nothing to be down about.

When Rita was in her early thirties, she consulted me because of depression and despair of her repeated miserable relationships with men. She longed for a good man to find her or for her to discover him. The men she picked were not only not good enough, they were bad and she knew it.

Rita kept a diary by her bed and every morning wrote her dream if she remembered it. One night during a torrential rainstorm, Rita had a strange dream that she was anxious to tell me:

Prologue:

I am worried about the rainstorm. I know that our house is above the flood plain but I don't feel completely safe. It sounds peculiar, but I am standing on the high foundation of our house looking into the backyard. In the distance, I see the rising river beyond the big trees in the backyard. I remember that the city is going to saw these trees down, but nobody seemed distressed by this. Suddenly I see my father in the backyard. He lunges into one of the big trees and it topples over. There are no roots.

Stormy weather – Nature is in an angry, wild state, over which no one has control. Rita comments on her parents' foresight in building a home above the flood plain but yet she feared the river would flood. She speaks of the "high foundation" of her childhood home. The shelter of the house was gone, however. The unusual phrase *high foundation* implies a solid, high base or footing. I was surprised by the news that no one protested when the city decided to cut down the big trees in the backyard. A human indifference to growing nature, a bureaucratic decision imposed upon an indifferent public. The surprisingly violent action by Rita's father does what the storm might have done, since the trees had no roots.

The dream story reveals her father lunging at the trees, doing by force what the impersonal city wanted to do: something bad, something brutal. The dream, considered from the perspective of the young woman's real-life crisis, might be a corrective to Rita's conscious admiration of her father, thus freeing her to find the gentleman she sought.

How might this dream help with the moral decision about the right thing to do? It seems to tell Rita that she, like the trees, needed roots in the earth so she is not toppled in the wind, or that she might stand up to her powerful father. Beneath the wonderful image of her childhood's wealthy persona was the image of the negative family values she ought to leave behind.

The dream continues:

> *The scene changes and I am visiting my mother's mother. She is very old and I have neglected her. She is on fire but shows no pain. Through the flames, my grandmother hands me her necklace with two small diamonds but I see that grandmother is wearing a huge diamond necklace and a string of beautiful pearls. All I can think of is how much I want them. Grandmother is dying in the fire, and when she is dead and the flames are gone, I take the huge diamond necklace and the pearls and put them on me and look in the mirror. I see that the pearls are fake and I do not like the huge diamond necklace. I give the necklace to my father and am contented with the small diamond necklace.*

The story has revealed Rita in the mirror, her glorification of the fake pearls, and her greed for the huge diamonds. Moral issues of the story are overvaluing money – loving it instead of finding human love, renunciation of greed, and covetousness.

In the context of Rita's real life, her decisions will be clearer when she has undistorted values.

In a nutshell: Simple values are more valuable than dazzling treasures.

Making a Choice:

The Dangerous Crossing

The following dream came to me at a time when I was encountering hostile opposition and resistance to setting up a new treatment program that I proposed. Practically, it was necessary for me to stand up and speak up for myself and my ideas and not to be passive. The outcome was uncertain, but the way to go was clear to me. If I stopped blaming the others and myself, the way to overcome the impasse would be more likely to present itself.

I have made the point earlier that it is impossible to create a value-free analysis or therapy without making right and wrong judgments. If people believe that they make no judgments, then patients will always know better, even if they remain silent out of deference to your belief system. The idea that we must be tentative about any blame leads to some odd behavior.

I remember a Stanford psychiatric resident reporting a therapy house to me for supervision in which the patient raged at him, calling him all sorts of bad names in a tirade of anger. He told me his response to his patient's attack: "Could it be that maybe, perhaps, you are angry with me?" The resident never got the point when I suggested that under the circumstances it would have been appropriate to say, "You are very mad at me. Tell me why."

His namby-pamby technique was only an exaggeration of what I call the Cult of the Tentative. I have no doubt that my anger at him got through, but as a supervisor I felt I ought not tell him that. This type of case calls for more straight-talk psychology. That and silent listening are good ways through hostility. Blaming is hostile; judgment per se is not.

Here is the dream I had:

> *It is night and I am crossing a long narrow bridge high in the air. It is only wide enough for one person. I could see ahead that the bridge was unfinished. It came to an abrupt end, suspended midway across a deep valley.*
> *I heard a buzzing sound at my right side. I looked down and realized that the sound came from electrical wires strung along the bridge, ending at a single unlit electric bulb. Next I discovered a switchbox by my right side. If I turned it one way, the light would go on. If I turned it the other way, some force would extend the bridge to the other side of the valley. A wind began to blow and the bridge swayed dangerously in the air. I knew that I would have to open the switchbox and make a choice about which way to turn the switch. I opened it up and to my surprise found a beautiful jewel.*

The setting: I am standing on an unfinished bridge. The dream question is now how I got there, but rather what is the meaning of my being suspended in midair on an unfinished bridge?

The buzzing is an alarm calling my attention to a switch with only two ways to turn it. Being in the dark of night in a tight spot just wide enough for one person, I had a decision to make about whether to turn on the light of present consciousness or power to the future – the other side of the valley. It could not be both. Crossing the bridge in such a powerfully dramatic situation is the archetypal story from one place to another, a metaphor for temporal life's beginning to end, birth to death.

The decision was how to use the energy that accompanied my crossing. A second alarm appears in the wind that emphasizes the danger of delaying the decision. The wind gives me a hint about which of the two decisions would be better. In a life-and-death situation with a possible long fall, Nature seems to be making its point about the need for stabilization and going. Once I take the action of opening the box, the story becomes like a fairy tale. The mechanical problem was miraculously transformed into a hidden treasure. As is often the case, the quester finds the jewel in an unexpected place – right where he is standing.

This is how I processed my dream.

Epictetus (*Manual: 5*) wrote that

> ... *when we are hindered or distressed, let us never lay blame on others, but on ourselves, that is, our own judgment. To accuse others for one's misfortune is a sign of want of education; to accuse oneself shows that one's education has begun; to accuse neither oneself nor others shows that one's education is complete.*

Leaving and Going On:

Stepping from Yesterday into Today

Change of work roles, change of jobs, and change of careers are major stresses that people experience. Longshoreman philosopher Eric Hoffer wrote a book titled *The Ordeal of Change*, telling how even a small change in a work pattern can be a big ordeal. The emotions and thoughts activated at these times reawaken power-loaded early memories of dramatic life changes. Dormant thoughts and fears about the future and death are evoked.

When one becomes old, changes may occur less often, but be more dramatic and difficult. Not only is it the experience of change that is always an ordeal, but also how this alteration may change values and even the meaning of your life. It may result in physical illness or psychological disorders.

Normal life crises are birth, adolescence, marriage, childhood, sickness, and death and are conceived of as the rites of passage. Dreams can help you make a moral decision that will affect the rest of your life. Try to think of your life story as a career in which there are crucial points where we must make specific decisions that identify our role, purpose, relative power, prestige, and influence. All changes can be thought of as life stages manifested by rites of passage. Social and cultural rites exist, in a large measure, to assure order, obedience, and levels of control in light of an organizing power that is beyond conscious control.

In Jungian psychology, this higher, supraordinate organiz-ing principle is the Self or *imago Dei* (image of God). Our ego and consciousness are subordinate to the Self. Change in Jungian psychology is associated with the mythology of trans-formation. It is symbolically lived through initiations permit-ting one to pass through a transition threshold and enter a new realm of the psyche. Monumental moments in life gener-ally awaken the unconscious to create dreams or nightmares portraying inner chaos, disorder, and demonic or beneficent helpful animals and human beings.

At times of change-of-life roles, we may fear that we have lost meaning in life, and suffer anxiety, fear, panic, dread, anger, depression – even suicidal ideas. To ignore dreams is not to look at the psychic traffic lights during rush hour.

People who bring me dreams at moments of major role change are aware of their general meaning, but lack the ability to see patterns in the disconnected parts of the dream. Over-view comprehension is rarely possible when one is in the midst of a potentially dangerous situation. I believe that it is wrong (my judgment) to take a dream literally in making decisions. Dreams do not tell us what to do. They inform us about conflicts so that we can make our own decisions. I would encourage people to ask their psyches for dreams if they want wise help from the depths of their souls, and are willing to take personal responsibility for their subsequent decision.

This idea is the thesis of my book: You can, you must, and you usually do make moral judgments. If you are fortunate enough to remember a dream at a time of crisis, and you pay serious attention to it, chances are that it will help you make the decision that is right for you.

Relinquishing Power: Stepping Down

As I mentioned previously, I knew it was right for me to retire when I was eighty years of age and become emeritus president and director of the Institute for the Humanities at Salado that I had founded almost two decades earlier. The institute had been a remarkable achievement. My successor was found. I felt good, following the maxim of Zen philosophy that one of the most important things in life is to know when to stop. One of my board members said, "One should leave before the party is over."

When I relinquished the power that I had held tightly in my hands, I naturally felt the sad feelings of separation, like the loss of a child I had brought into existence. The child, however, was grown up, healthy, and strong. The members of the institute constituted a loyal, caring, and grateful family For seventeen years, the atmosphere of the institute was marked by the best of Texan hospitality and a satisfying civility. I was passing its total direction to another person who would conduct the institute according to his own style and personality.

For the first months of transition, I felt genuine joy to have found a highly qualified successor, and relief of the burdens of the operation of the institute. Then strong feelings emerged. Some disagreements arose. Now was the time to relinquish power, not to control that which I had given to someone else to carry out.

I have had years of experience in treating men and women who have retired or moved on, stepped down, or stepped up from positions of power. I had learned from that rich experience that all their transitions were painful and carried with them both sadness and joy. I had listened carefully to their dreams.

A series of dreams and nightmares guided me through these troubling times, offering wisdom, bringing tranquillity, and suggesting moral counsel. I typed out my dream every morning and analyzed it every evening. The dream scenarios were extraordinarily powerful. I will tell you one of my early dreams.

Part I: A Silent Dignified Exit

I am sitting on the aisle of the back row, on the left side of a large auditorium. A speaker on the podium is presenting a paper. At the end of the lecture, I see that my father is sitting on the right side in the center of the last row. He is handsome and impressive. His face and presence are strong and kind. He shows the best of my father's qualities. I am very happy to be near him. At the end of the performance, there is applause. The time has come to leave the auditorium, but my father lingers there with some of his friends as the audience walks out. I watch across the aisle that separates my father and me. Finally I decide that it is time to leave, and I walk out alone.

It is unusual for me to dream of my dead father as such a positive figure. He is close but we are separated, and he is with his friends. In the dream, I am surprised and very happy that he is there. He looks to me like the proverbial Grand Old Man, but about fifty years old. It is as if he had come back to show me something of value. My name is Harry A. Wilmer II, and his friends have frequently commented on our resemblance. Even in the dream, I was aware that I looked like him. Perhaps his presence reminded me of my more youthful side but still being the old man in the back row near the exit. My father lingers around after the performance, visiting with his friends.

That part of me remains in the theater even after the end, when the other part leaves alone.

The dream setting reveals the institute lectures continuing without me. I am out of the limelight and quite contented. What will the dream reveal after this satisfied, happy episode? The dream's motif is about a public persona; it is well to remember that behind the persona hides the shadow.

The dream continues:

Part II: Serious Danger Lurks

I walk into my bedroom and find three or four ominous men dressed in black. I know they are terrorists.

The dream setting has shifted from a collective theater t my personal space. Why have these dangerous criminal figures appeared after the contented previous episode? I think they appear to remind me that the shadow of my *good* father is my *bad* father, and to make me see both sides.

My identification with my father forces me to face my own threatening shadow after the applause for an outstanding performance. Behind the face of tranquillity lurks terror.

The dream continues:

One of the terrorists assaults me while the others stand by watching. I cannot get rid of the aggressive man. Wherever I try to go, he is there. I note that he has a revolver in his left hand. The most striking feature is his persona – a totally black cloak, and a partial black head mask which covers his head. In the front of the black face mask is a narrow open slit over the chin, mouth, and nose that opens out in a T-pattern with wider space over both eyes. This configuration gives the impression of a knight's face armor in the Middle Ages, perhaps a crusader whom I am fighting and from whom I am trying to escape.

This shadow episode tells me that I must be on guard against the deceptive nature of the good persona. I must be aware of the positive and not overlook the negative. When institutions and people look great, there are always lurking shadows. That is the nature of humanity. Danger rests in power. Given this scenario, will the dream now show me how to cope with this cliffhanger?

The dream continues:

Part III: Down the Up Elevator

I find myself on the top floor of a large university building. I am trying to get down to the ground floor and go home. Although I am already returned from the university and have gone back for a visit, I do not see anyone. I cannot decide which of two elevators to take down. One of them goes down very fast, but instead of stopping on the ground floor turns at a right angle and zooms into the country for miles before stopping. The other elevator stops at each floor. Which elevator is which? There are no signs.

The scene shows me in the role of the returning professor to visit my old haunt, but no one is there. So I must come down from a high place to the ground. My father and I were also high in the theater – the back row.

The dream concludes:

Part IV: A Grotesque Woman Appears

I encounter a tall obese naked woman with large breasts and stomach. She is pursuing me and is sex crazy, like a nymphomaniac. I am trying to get away from her.

Before I was trying to get away from the aggressive man; now I am trying to get away from the aggressive woman. The masculine principle was power gone wild. The feminine principle was eros gone wild. She was the grotesque witch out to get me. Technical aspects of transportation were not the problem; it was the negative side of human nature.

Inner Value/Outer Value:

The Hidden Treasure

We cannot live by external values alone, nor by internal values alone. There are critical times in our lives when it is necessary to decide which one we should choose to be our preference. The moral position is not about relative values or absolute values, but rather about the basis upon which we make choices.

I will tell you two final dreams from last week. They appear while I am writing this book and thinking of how it will play with me, with you, and with a collective audience. The two dreams occurred on consecutive nights.

I experienced them as symbolic gifts from my unconscious. On the day before the first dream, I had made an important decision that liberated me from burdens that would interfere with my determination to devote the major part of the rest of my life to writing.

The First Dream: A Big Show

I have been invited to give a lecture in a large university auditorium. I walk in and see that all the seats are taken. I become extremely anxious because I have not prepared a speech. There is no escape so I walk to the podium, afraid that I will make a fool of myself. Once I stand behind the lectern, I decide on the spot to present my talk by telling dreams in a new and dramatic way so that they become living histories. After the talk, I will ask members of the

audience direct and penetrating questions. Now that I am feeling in control, my fear disappears and I begin my talk.
I hear a racket coming from high in the back of the auditorium and look up to see many boisterous high school students celebrating with total indifference to the program. They are joking and talking loudly. To make matters worse, their high school band in bright uniforms begins to play. I stop the program, and order all of these youngsters to leave the auditorium. They instantly become quiet and file out the back doors.

The dream shows how I want to keep my own center and not be disrupted by external things that are not helpful. I am not prepared for a big extraverted performance. The dream idea on which I want to lecture in the essence of this book. I am confident and take charge once I make that decision. The rowdy voices and band in the back are the workings of my mind that divert me from my task. All I have to do is to stand up and speak out. This action is the masculine authority that will protect me and give me a more quiet life. I woke up feeling quite happy. Silencing the extraverted noisy world made sense. What will the next performance show?

Next Night: The Second Dream –
Discovering the Right Values

I enter a beautiful home furnished in the classical style of a wealthy old family. Standing in the living room is a striking-ly beautiful young woman. On the wall directly behind her hangs a large oil painting. I do not see the picture but it is in a handsome gold frame. Without either of us saying a word, she turns and slides the painting to the side revealing a vault in the wall. She opens it, takes out a treasure, and gives it to me.

This dream is short and sweet. It was not an erotic dream, though it would be simple to make a sexual interpretation. It was instead the image of a majestically beautiful woman guide. There is something more precious behind that beauty. The room, the woman, and the painting created an aesthetic impression, a persona. It is conventional to say that behind the persona is the shadow. Not here – for hidden behind the outer beauty, deep within, is the treasure. The woman plays the role of leading me to it and opening it up. That I do not see the treasure adds to the mystery, but clearly it is the object of greater value than the extraverted values on public display. The real value is the inner value. Like an explorer, I am looking for deeper meanings than meet the eye.

The dream is affirmation of my quest and a hint not to be concerned with the noisy voices of critics. I asked them out in the first dream and moved on to the heart of the matter where the feminine and the masculine are in balance.

Living in the Present:

A Hic et Nunc Dream

What is more present than last night's dream? In completing this book, I thought I needed a final dream. Last night in my greenhouse, I was reading about the Arctic in preparation for our trip to Spitsbergen near the North Pole. For the past twenty-six years, Jane and I have gone to Switzerland but now is a time to take a new venture before it is too late. Last night I was thinking about C. A. Meier, my Jungian analyst in Zurich in 1970. I spent hours telling him about my childhood. Isn't that what you are supposed to do? Isn't that why I spent years on a Freudian couch?

One day, in exasperation, Meier suddenly burst out with two Latin words: *"Hic et Nunc!"* The tone of voice came over like a command, most unusual for this patient, intelligent, very introverted man. I knew the words meant "here and now" because he had often said to me, "Focus on the here and now." This day I had wandered off into history and the collective unconscious, probably trying to impress him. He gave me a moral directive to come back down to earth from the heights of Jungian archetypal and esoteric thought, and examine the immediacy of life in the context of my last dreams.

This is last night's dream:

Entrance and Exit:
A Message of Hope

Prologue: Unexpected Visit of the Sailors

I have a new home. It is smaller and simpler than my present home and has the pleasant feeling of being new and immaculately clean. There is not a speck of dust to be seen. I know that a camera crew is going to come here later today to make a documentary film. Sitting directly across from me are two American sailors dressed in old-fashioned uniforms with large broad collars and big bow ties. We sit in silence for a long time. I am trying to ignore them.

This house is in Minneapolis, near where I lived as a child, and represents *home*. I know that I must speak with the sailors because they have come to talk with me. What message will they bring? It was pleasant seeing them sitting here because of my wonderful memories of the navy. There is an air of mystery in the room.

When I was in the navy, the Pacific Naval Combat Crew filmed my experimental ward for one month. A major docudrama was later made for commercial television. Last week I had a phone call from Stephen Segallar telling me that he would be sending me the completed film documentary on the Salado institute with Bill Moyers's narration. These events affect the prologue. It has an air of pleasant mystery, but what message is going to be delivered to me?

The dream continues:

I reach over the table and offer my hand to the sailor across from me, introducing myself. He tells me he has wanted to meet me for a long time and that he knew my mother. In some way, that explained how he got entry into my house, although I knew my mother was dead. The second sailor fades from the dream, bringing focus on the first one. He is anxious to tell me that the president had changed the structure of the navy by only selecting officers who were

*anthropologists and archaeologists. He has heard that I am
discouraged by how the navy is deteriorating and wants to
bring me this wonderful news. In the dream, I am aware
that there is a hidden wisdom in this change, a totally new
way to prepare for conflict or war.*

I was intrigued by this news. While it made no logical sense,
it had a profound symbolic significance in the transformation
of a fighting heroic young military force into one dominated
by deep thought, science, and the humanities. Archaeologists
patiently dig to discover hidden secrets of the past, but what
did this have to do with me, personally, when my direction is
to be *hic et nunc*?

The dream continues:

*The sailor is standing in the front doorway of my house,
preparing to leave. He no longer wears a sailor suit but a
smart khaki explorer's uniform with no military insignia,
and bears no arms. He wears a broad-brimmed Aussie hat
and is ready to travel to the interior of Africa. He says that
in the war he had seen Auschwitz and many terrible hap-
penings so he is eager to change things, and to take on his
new military diplomatic mission.*

*He stands there in silence for a moment – handsome, in a
grand posture reminding me of Sir Laurens van der Post
when he came back from being a prisoner of war of the
Japanese in Java. Against orders, he stopped off in the
African jungle to be with the animals, especially to come
close to a white rhinoceros. He did. They stared at each
other and finally the rhinoceros walked away.*

The dream is as if I am given a picture framed in a doorway
of my friend transformed into the awesome van der Post. I had
van der Post especially in mind because of his plans to visit me
in Salado before his death. Figuratively speaking, he has sent
an emissary in the dream who embodies the prime of young
patriotic manhood about to embark on a heroic life.

As van der Post grew older, he devoted himself to writing and creating a humanities foundation in London. He is remembered for being a brilliant, gentle, and wise man, who loved to tell stories of the African natives. A novelist who saw life as story, he was always telling people stories. Van der Post wrote a book and made a BBC documentary film about C. G. Jung. He was a world-famous man, a hero who never succumbed to hubris.

Another Dream Follows with the Moral

> *I am at a large party talking with another doctor who practices internal medicine. Someone runs up to us and says that a guest has gone to the parking lot and collapsed. We run outside. The other doctor examines the man and says he is dead. I recognize the dead man as a friend of mine, a retired army officer who is suffering from Alzheimer's disease. In the dream, I cannot recall his name because my memory is slipping. I call him General Grant (Ulysses S. Grant). I examine the body to assure myself that he is dead. To everyone's surprise, I say, "There must be some way to bring him back to life. Call 911."*
> *An ambulance arrives and I go with the body to a busy hospital emergency room. In some spectacular and strange way, I bring him back to life while the other doctors in the ER watch with astonishment. I begin bragging about my career in medicine. The other doctors look on with indifference. A psychiatrist friend whom I have known since the 1940s, now gray haired and old, walks up and warns me, "Don't carry on so much about yourself, saying that you were once a pathologist at Johns Hopkins. No one cares!" I know he is right and I shut up.*

I come to the obvious moral decision: Do not try to bring dead war heroes with Alzheimer's back to life. And from an ethical standpoint, do not be like the doctors who must resort to miserable heroic measures trying to defeat death. We should accept that we must let some people die, as they say, "with dignity," and to accept our own deaths with the same philosophies by which we have lived our lives and by which we must die our deaths. The hero motif belongs naturally in the first half of life. Just before van der Post died at ninety, he had instructed his publisher to send me a copy of his last book, *The Admiral's Baby*, about his heroic experiences in Java after the Japanese defeat. His face on the jacket looks like the soldier standing in my dream doorway.

For myself, the moral is to keep life simple, avoid the heroic life, and settle for the arts and sciences – especially for writing.

Notes

1. Freud identified the *superego* as the source of conscience which keeps watch over actions and intentions of the ego and judges them by exercising censorship. The purpose of dream censorship was to hide objectionable ideas, "so that a penis may be represented by a snake, ape, hat, or airplane. Dream symbols are a tool of dream censorship." Freud said the dream censorship led to secondary psychological revision of dreams; therefore, dreams were the guardians of sleep, and every successful dream was a fulfillment of that wish.

At the present time, most Freudians have discarded the dream censorship and guardian of sleep concepts. His original thesis ascribed a distinct moral purpose to dreams.

Freud wrote:

> I have isolated from the subject the special problem of whether and to what extent moral dispositions and feelings extend into dream-life. ... Some [authors] assert that the dictates of morality have no place in dreams, while others maintain no less positively that the moral character of man persists in his dream-life. "Ap-

peal to the common experience of dreams seems to establish beyond any doubt the correctness of the former of these views." (p. 66)

On the inconsistencies of the authors whom Freud cited, he said:

Those who maintain that the moral personality of man ceases to operate in dreams should, in strict logic, lose all interest in immoral dreams. They could rule out any attempt at holding a dreamer responsible for his dreams, or at deducing from the wickedness of his dreams that he had an evil streak in his character, just as confidently as they would reject a similar attempt at deducing from the absurdity of his dreams that his intellectual activities in waking life were worthless. The other group, who believe that the "categorical imperative" extends to dreams, should logically accept responsibility for immoral dreams. We could only hope for their sake that they would have no such reprehensible dreams of their own to upset their firm belief in their own moral character. ... It appears, however, that no one is as confident as all that of how far he is good or bad, and no one can deny the recollection of immoral dreams of his own. (p. 68)

Many writers, Freud said, have contradictory opinions on the moral issue of dreams, and comes to the conclusion:

We may, then, class together under the heading "involuntary ideas" the whole of the ideational material the emergence of which, like in immoral and in absurd dreams, cause us so much bewilderment. There is, however, one important point of difference: involuntary ideas in the moral sphere contradict our usual attitude of mind, whereas the others merely strike us as strange. No step has yet been taken toward a deeper knowledge which would resolve this distinction. (p. 71)

Dreams of being naked or insufficiently dressed in the presence of strangers sometimes occur with the additional feature of there being a complete absence of any such feeling as shame on the dreamer's part. We are only concerned here, however, with those ideas of being naked in which one *does* feel shame and embarrassment and tries to escape or hide, and is then overcome by a strange inhibition which prevents one from moving and makes one feel incapable of altering one's distressing situation. It is only with this accompaniment that the dream is typical; without it, the gist of the subject-matter may be included in every variety of context or be ornamented with individual trimmings. (p. 242)

2. Narrative and Imagination: In a way, I am not the author of this book but the narrator. Lamarque and Olsen, in a monograph entitled *Truth, Fiction, and Literature*, say:

> ... that what a narrative is about, cannot be determined independently of how the subject-matter is presented (the structural dimension), and for what purpose (the genre dimension). ... Narratives inevitably distort what they portray and thus, again, the manner of presentation is not independent of the matter presented. ... Narratives of necessity have narrators (real or implied) and narrators occupy some point of view on what they narrate; they also select the material, assigning weight to some aspects, playing down others, leaving out some matters altogether; they structure events in temporal and causal relations and the order of narration need not reflect the order of occurrence; they address a particular kind of reader (or audience); they use a particular kind of vocabulary, often redolent with connotations, and commonly adopt a stance, or attitude towards the events narrated.

Lamarque and Olsen cite various views on the nature of narrative: (1) It plays a central, even indispensable, role in cognition. (2) It is a primary and irreducible form of human comprehension. (3) Narrative is a primary act of mind transferred to art from life itself. (4) Human beings have a fundamental disposition to organize experience narrationally, given that they are natural storytellers. (5) Our lives are ceaselessly intertwined with narrative and the stories we tell, and are reworked in the story of our lives that we narrate to ourselves. (6) A human being's identity is defined in terms of a life narrative to give order and purpose to one's life.

3. In 1945, Jung published a work called *On the Nature of Dreams*, asking himself, "To what purpose does it [the dream] happen?" He says:

> Of all psychic phenomena the dream presents the largest number of "irrational" factors. It seems to possess a minimum of that logical coherence and that hierarchy of values shown by other contents of consciousness, and is therefore less transparent and understandable. Dreams that form logically, morally, or aesthetically satisfying wholes are exceptional. Usually a dream is a strange and disconcerting product distinguished by many "bad qualities," such as lack of logic, questionable morality, uncouth form, and apparent absurdity or nonsense. People are therefore only too glad to dismiss it as stupid, meaningless and worthless. (Para. 532)

Every interpretation of a dream is a psychological statement about certain of its contents. This is not without danger, as the dreamer, like most people, usually displays an astonishing sensitivity to critical remarks, not only if they are wrong, but even more if they are right. Since it is not possible, except under very special conditions, to work out the meaning of a dream without the collaboration of the dreamer, an extraordinary amount of tact is required not to violate his self-respect unnecessarily. (Para. 533)

Jung had the following to say on drama and narrative in dreams:

Coming now to the form of dreams, we find everything from lightning impressions to endlessly spun out dream-narrative. Nevertheless there are a great many "average" dreams in which a definite structure can be perceived, not unlike that of a drama. For instance, the dream begins with A STATEMENT OF PLACE. Next comes a statement about the PROTAGONISTS. ... Statements of time are rare. [The next] phase of the dream, the EXPOSITION, indicates the scene of action, the people involved, and often the initial situation of the dreamer.

In the second phase comes the DEVELOPMENT of the plot. ... The situation is somehow becoming complicated and a definite tension develops because one does not know what will happen.

The third phase brings in the CULMINATION or perepetia. Here something decisive happens or something changes completely. ...

The fourth and last phase is the lysis, the SOLUTION OR RESULT produced by the dream-work. There are certain dreams in which the fourth phase is lacking. ... (Para. 561-64)

4. Whitmont and Perera, in writing about the dramatic structure of the dream, state that the motif of theater is an archetypal representation of the psyche's mythopoetic activity, which equates existence with dramatic performance. They cite Jung's four structural elements and add:

Every dream opens with some problematic situation that is brought to the viewer's attention by the exposition, a *setting* in a particular time and space with particular characters. This states the theme of the play and orients the viewers to that author's perspective on that theme. The problematic situation often refers to some issue that is stuck or fixated, and which presents the starting point for the ensuing development. In a dream we usually

find what the problematic issue is by examining the opening setting of the dream. This means exploring the psychological meaning of the affect-laden associations and explanations that are
connected with the dream's particular location in time and space
as well as the qualities of the particular people present, and their
relationship to the dreamer. All of this conveys the psychologi-
cal/symbolic context or focus of the dream. Stating the theme or
the problem with which the dream deals, then, is the task of the
dream's exposition. The *exposition states the theme.* We may
compare it with a business bulletin's or form letter's superscrip-
tion, "Re:" which means "referring to" and which states the basic
subject matter of the communication – that is, appointments,
personnel, scheduling, or whatever. (pp. 67-78)

The authors present and discuss dream from the perspective of
the four structures. They give specific clinical details of the patient's
life and analysis, and summarize, for example:

Whereas the setting pointed to the past roots of the present problem, the development shows the current movement or tendencies arising from the problem and leading to a stalemate or
threatening impasse. The crisis is the high point at which conflicting forces are most tensely opposed and at which a decision
or turn of events, one way or another, must occur. The crisis may
be said to show present and future. It shows what the development is aiming at or is already in the process of establishing. In
this dream ... the crisis occurs when she cannot get help from the
police, the collective guardian of law and order. The police's
function is to enforce a generally valid, not an individual, principle of order. ...

The dream shows us where we are, how we may be amiss, and
what possibilities are open to us; but unless we also attempt to
test those ways of going with them and wrestling with their dif-
ficulties, the dream message is in vain.

5. Bert States's 1993 book *Dreaming and Storytelling* presents
theoretical and psychological aspects of dream narration, fiction,
storytelling. and dreams in literature. His chapter "Meaning in
Dreams and Fiction" focuses on the theoretical construct of intentionality of the dream. Taken from the point of view of a deconstructionist, he concludes that dreams are basically meaningless. He
discusses the idea of meaning of dreams themselves not in the
context of being related to a real person. When a dream is told to
another person in the psychologic process of seeking understanding
or relief of suffering, the dream is not an isolated thing. It is rare that

a dream can be understood without the patient's participation. It is essentially the dialogue between patient and dream interpreter that creates meaning.

Experience tells me that telling of one's dream to another individual, and that person attentive enough to remember it, can elicit unsuspected meaning for the dreamer. This situation can occur without a response from the other provided that he/she is listening with total attention. In my own practice, I see that the healing impact of dream work is enhanced when I can retell the dream to the dreamer to clarify and connect. I am always ready to be corrected about elements I have forgotten or misunderstood. Then we are both talking about the same dream images and story.

States says that the theoretical construct in the analyst's mind accounts for his or her interpretation. This conclusion seems self-evident, but that does not invalidate the meaning. By the same token, the deconstructionist's theoretical construct of meaninglessness of life and dream phenomena accounts for his finding the dream meaningless.

It is in the psychic rough and tumble of analytic work with the irrational unconscious world, not in rational intellectual thinking, that real-life meaning can be found. I have presented selected dreams in narrative story form in the manner that I was first engaged with them. The meanings evolved from our dialogue plus my understanding of the dreamer's life and tensions. When I approach a dream with the questions in my mind: "How can this dream help this person?" and "Is there a clue to resolve a moral indecision?" – the way I am dealing with dreams relates to the intentionality of the listener, not the dream.

States begins the chapter "Meaning in Dreams and Fictions" with these words:

> Behind our preoccupation with meaning in dreams lurks an implication that they must be rescued from the threat of meaninglessness. ... The problem with dreaming is that there is no apparent receiver and hence the whole dimension of intentionality – one of subconditions of meaning – acquires a questionable status. (pp. 140-41)

Is it not apparent that the receiver of the dream is the dreamer – and if the dreamer is in analysis, that the nature of transference creates a second apparently intended receiver, the analyst?

States raises the issue of truth in the meaning of dreams:

I have doubts about whether the interpretive switch within the allegorical text is, after all, the same as the switch from dream-as-dreamt to waking interpreter. Isn't the latter a switch from experience to interpretation involving two entirely different classes of truth that may determine very different kinds of meanings? And if one uses an exterior class of truth (or system of meanings) to interpret the interior dream-as-dreamt, is this not in effect to privilege one form of truth over another, and the theory that the dream, as a consequence of censorship [sic], has less access to its *true associations and context* than the waking interpreter? (p. 148, my emphasis)

Perhaps dreams are, after all, only a kind of psychic digestive system, with no more awareness of what they are doing than the stomach. (p. 150)

This reductive analysis of dreaming to a physiological basis ignores the gross, microscopic, and molecular biophysiology of the stomach, which is not a dumb container. I have treated a Vietnam war veteran whose war nightmare was so sickening that he woke up in a sweat and vomited repeatedly. I did not make the common cliché interpretation that "he could not stomach his dream," or a mystical interpretation about "the wisdom of the stomach," because "being sick to the stomach" struck me as a natural reaction to seeing a catastrophic trauma. It is pathophysiological, as natural as its physiological digestive function.

It is awkward but natural to say that *States states* that our theoretical expectations dictate what we are able to say about a dream, just as they dictate what we say about art, and that there are four dominant interpretive methodologies in literature and dreams: psychoanalytic, semiotic, phenomenologic, and structural (p. 180). He embraces the *deconstructive approach*, a theoretical approach which expects the world and dreams to be meaningless.

Psychiatrists are referred to the following articles:

Kramer, M., R. Whitman, B. Baldridge, and L. Lansky, "Patterns of Dreaming: The Interrelationship of the Dreams of the Night" in *Journal of Nervous and Mental Diseases*, 139 (1964), 426-39.

Kramer, M., R. Hlasny, G. Jacobs, and T. Roth, "Do Dreams Have Meaning: An Empirical Inquiry" in *American Journal of Psychiatry*, 133: 778-81.

The Last Word

SHE: "You say that my dreams can help me make a moral decision. Right?"

HE: "Wrong!"

SHE: "Wrong?"

HE: "*Sometimes* wrong. If you think that *any* of your dreams will work, you're wrong. If you think that *certain* of your dreams will work, you are right. Does that sound right?"

SHE: "Right *and* wrong. I'm not certain."

HE: "We are only certain for fleeting moments. Now I think I have made my point."

SHE: "Wrong!"

HE: "Wrong?"

SHE: "*Sometimes* wrong."

HE: "Sometimes *right*. Does that settle the issue?"

SHE: "I'll tell you in the morning – if I have the *right* kind of dream."

HE: (Silence)

SHE: "Good night."

List of Characters:

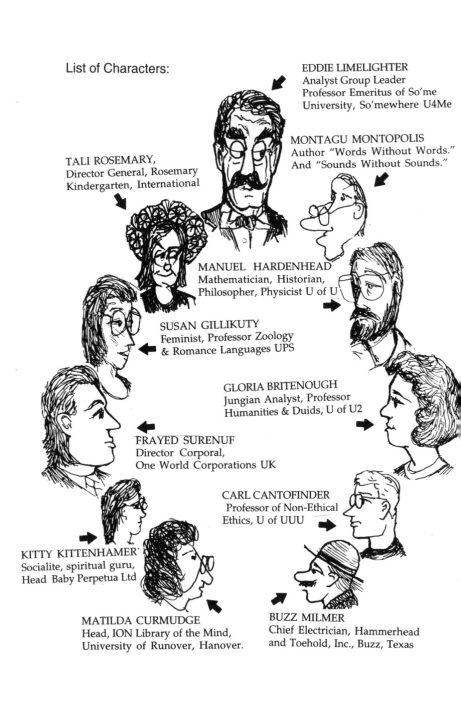

EDDIE LIMELIGHTER
Analyst Group Leader
Professor Emeritus of So'me
University, So'mewhere U4Me

MONTAGU MONTOPOLIS
Author "Words Without Words."
And "Sounds Without Sounds."

TALI ROSEMARY,
Director General, Rosemary
Kindergarten, International

MANUEL HARDENHEAD
Mathematician, Historian,
Philosopher, Physicist U of U

SUSAN GILLIKUTY
Feminist, Professor Zoology
& Romance Languages UPS

GLORIA BRITENOUGH
Jungian Analyst, Professor
Humanities & Duids, U of U2

FRAYED SURENUF
Director Corporal,
One World Corporations UK

CARL CANTOFINDER
Professor of Non-Ethical
Ethics, U of UUU

KITTY KITTENHAMER
Socialite, spiritual guru,
Head Baby Perpetua Ltd

MATILDA CURMUDGE
Head, ION Library of the Mind,
University of Runover, Hanover.

BUZZ MILMER
Chief Electrician, Hammerhead
and Toehold, Inc., Buzz, Texas

Appendix

Although dreams disclose the unconscious to us with perhaps the truest approach to faithfulness we can attain, we also come upon its traces in every form of creative activity, such as music and poetry; and in all kinds of art. It appears in all manifestations of a spontaneous and creative kind, the further these are removed from everything mechanical, technical, and intellectual.
     – C. G. Jung (1943)

Bibliography

Introduction

Brodzky, Ann, et. al., *Stones, Bones and Skin: Ritual and Shamanic Art* (Toronto: Society for Graphic Arts Publications, 1971).

Daoren, Huanchu, *Back to Beginnings: Reflections on the Tao (1600).* (Boston: Shambhala, 1990), 6.

Part I: POWER

Almond, Barbara, and Richard Almond, *The Therapeutic Narrative: Fictional Relationships and the Process of Psychological Change* (Westport, Conn.: Praeger, 1996), 138, 146.

Green, Julien., *God's Fool: The Life and Times of Francis of Assisi* (New York: Harper and Row, 1985),119, 120-21.

Haggard, Rider, *She.*

Hillman, James, "The Fiction of Case History: A Round," chap. 5 in *Religion as Story*, edited by James B. Wiggins (New York: Harper and Row, 1975), 124, 133-34, 155, 157, 159.

Hillman, James, *Healing Fiction* (Woodstock, Conn.: Spring Publications, 1983), 35-36, 55, 129.

Jones, A. Hudson, "Psychiatrists on Broadway (1974-1982)" in *Literature and Medicine, Vol. 4: Psychiatry and Literature*, edited by P. W. Graham (Baltimore: Johns Hopkins University Press, 1985), 128-39.

Jung, C.G., "A Psychological View of Conscience," in *Collected Works, 2nd ed., Vol. 10: Civilization in Transition* (Princeton, N.J.: Princeton University Press, 1970), Para. 826.

Kyokai, Bukkyo Dendo, *The Teaching of Buddha* (Tokyo: Kosaido Printing, 1966), 378.

Moffitt, Alan; Milton Kramer; and Robert Hoffman (eds.) *The Functions of Dreaming* (State University of New York Press, 1993).

Pascal, Blaise, *Pensées, IV* in *Pascal's Pensées* (New York, Penguin Books, 1966).

Sandburg, Carl, *Abraham Lincoln: The Prairie Years and the War Years* (New York: Harcourt, Brace, 1954), 697-98.

Wilmer, Harry A., "Psychiatrist on Broadway," in *American Imago*, Vol. 12/2 (1955), 158-78.

Part II: EVIL

Grimm, Jacob, and Wilhelm Grimm, *The Brothers Grimm Fairy Tales: Everyman's Library* (New York: Knopf, 1992), 348-59.

Jung, C. G., "Good and Evil in Analytical Psychology" in *Collected Works, 2nd. ed., Vol. 10: Civilization in Transition* (Princeton, N.J.: Princeton University Press, 1970), 456-67.

_____, "Psychology and Religion" in *Collected Works, 2nd ed., Vol. 11: West and East* (Princeton, N.J.: Princeton University Press, 1969), Para. 134.

Moyers, Bill, "Facing Evil," PBS-TV documentary, 1988 (on the Salado symposium reported in the Woodruff and Wilmer book *Facing Evil*).

Nietzsche, Friedrich, *The Portable Nietzsche*, translated and edited by Walter Kaufmann (New York: Viking Press, 1954).

_____, *Beyond Good and Evil: Prelude to a Philosophy of the Future*, translated by Walter Kaufmann (New York: Vintage Books, 1966).

Sanford, Nevitt; Craig Comstock; and Associates, *Sanctions for Evil: Sources of Social Destructiveness* (Boston: Beacon Press, 1971), 60.

Wilmer, Harry A., "The Healing Nightmare: War Dreams of Vietnam Veterans," chapter 6 in *Trauma and Dreams* edited by Dierdre Barrett (Cambridge: Harvard University Press, 1996), 85-99.

_____, "The Healing Nightmare: A Study of the War Dreams of Vietnam Combat Veterans" in *Quadrant*, Spring 1986, 47-62.

Woodruff, Paul, and Harry A. Wilmer (eds.), *Facing Evil: Light at the Core of Darkness* (LaSalle, Ill.: Open Court, 1988).

Part III: WORLD-SHAKING DREAMS

Bunyan, John, *The Pilgrim's Progress: In a Similitude of a Dream* [1678] (New York: Dodd, Mead, 1979 ed.).

Foxe, John, *Book of Martyrs*,

Jung, C.G., "A Psychological View of Conscience" in *Collected Works, 2nd ed., Vol. 10: Civilization in Transition* (Princeton, N.J.: Princeton University Press, 1970), Para. 835.

Redfearn, J. W. T., "Dreams of Nuclear Warfare: Does Avoiding the Intrapsychic Clash of Opposites Contribute to the Concrete Danger of World Destruction?" in *Dreams in Analysis* edited by

N. Schwartz-Salant and Murray Stein (Wilmette, Ill,: Chiron, 1990), 181-98.

Soames, Mary, *Clementine Churchill: The Biography of a Marriage* (Boston: Houghton Mifflin, 1979), 134-35.

Wilmer, Harry A., *Huber the Tuber: Lives and Loves of a Tubercle Bacillus* (New York: American Tuberculosis Association, 1942).

_____, "Dream Seminar for Chronic Schizophrenic Patients" in *Psychiatry*, 45/4 (1982), 351-60.

_____, "The Healing Nightmare: War Dreams of Vietnam Veterans," chapter 6 in *Trauma and Dreams* edited by Deirdre Barrett (Cambridge: Harvard University Press, 1996).

Part IV: CONTROL OF THE MIND

Crick, F., and G. Mitchison, "The Function of Dream Sleep," *Nature*, Vol. 304/14 (July 1983), 111-14.

Darwin, Charles, *The Descent of Man and Selection in Relation to Sex* (New York: Modern Library, 1982), chapter 4.

Farber, C. M., and R. H. L. Wilson, *Control of the Mind: Man and Civilization* (New York: McGraw-Hill, 1961), based on a symposium held at the University of California Medical Center, San Francisco, January 28-30, 1961.

Jung, C. G., "Foreword to Perry: The Self in Psychotic Process" in *The Symbolic Life, Vol. 18: Collected Works* (Princeton, N.J.: Princeton University Press, 1976), 354-55.

Levi, Primo, *The Drowned and the Saved* (New York: Vintage Books, 1989), 31.

Maugham, Somerset, "Mr. Know It All" in

Meier, C. A., "Dramatic Structure of the Dream" in *The Meaning and Significance of Dreams* edited by (Boston: Sigo, 1987), 87-93.

Part V: GOOD

Darwin, Charles, *The Origin of Species* (Totowa, N.J.: Rowman and Littlefield, 1975).

Epictetus, *The Manuell of Epictetus: London, 1576* (Amsterdam: Theatrum Orbis Terrarum, 1977), 5.

Freud, Sigmund, "The Moral Sense in Dreams" in *The Interpretation of Dreams (First Part), Standard Ed. of the Complete Psychological Works of Sigmund Freud, Vol. IV (1900)* (London: Hogarth Press and the Institute of Psychoanalysis, 1953), 66-67.

Hoffer, Eric, *The Ordeal of Change*

Jung, C.G., "A Psychological View of Conscience" in *Collected Works, 2nd ed., Vol. 10: Civilization in Transition* (Princeton, N.J.: Princeton University Press, 1970), Para. 835.

_____, "On the Nature of Dreams" in *Collected Works of C. G. Jung, 2nd ed., Vol. 8: The Structure and Dynamics of the Psyche* (Princeton, N.J.: Princeton University Press, 1969), Para. 561-69.

Lamarque, P., and S. H. Olsen, *Truth, Fiction, and Literature: A Philosophical Perspective* (Oxford, England: Clarendon Press, 1994), 223, 235.

Moyers, Bill, Documentary on Institute for the Humanities at Salado

Sondheim, Stephen, *Sunday in the Park with George: A Musical* (New York: Dodd, Mead, 1986).

States, B. O., "Meaning in Dreams and Fictions," chapter 5 in *Dreaming and Storytelling* (Ithaca, N.Y.: Cornell University Press, 1993), 142-85.

Van der Post, Laurens, *The Admiral's Baby*

Whitmont, E. C., and S. B. Perera, "The Dramatic Structure of the Dream," chapter 7 in *Dreams: A Portal to the Source* (New York: Routledge, 1989), 67-78.

Wilmer, Harry A., *Silence* (Toronto: Inner City Books, in press).

_____, "The Meaning and Function of Dreams," Part VI in *Practical Jung: Nuts and Bolts of Jungian Psychotherapy* (Wilmette, Ill.: Chiron, 1987), 209-51.

_____, "Dreams," Parts VI, VII, and VIII in *Understandable Jung: The Personal Side of Jungian Psychology* (Wilmette, Ill.: Chiron, 1994), 88-162.

_____, "What Do You Say When a Patient Tells You a Dream?" in *Texas Medicine*, 78 (1982), 46-48.

References

5   De Tocqueville, Alexis, *Democracy in America*, edited by Richard Heffner (New York: Mentor Books, 1966).

9   Borges, Jorge Luis.

17   Howells, William Dean. (1895)

47   Milton, John, *Areopagitica* (Philadelphia: A. Saifer, 1972. English reprints, no. 1).

79   Montaigne, Michel de, *Essays I.xxi* (Stanford, Calif.: Stanford University Press, 1958).

103   Santayana, George, *Little Essays Drawn from the Writings of George Santayana* (Freeport, N.Y.: Books for Libraries Press, 1967).

139   Carroll, Lewis. *Alice's Adventures in Wonderland* (New York: Philomel Books, 1989), 90.

183   Jung, C. G. (1943)

About the Author

Harry Wilmer is founder, emeritus director, and president of the Institute for the Humanities at Salado, a small central Texas village where he has lived since 1971. Wilmer is a senior Jungian analyst in private practice in Salado, and spends mornings and evenings writing books, articles, and poetry, as well as illustrating his books.

He received his B.S., M.S., M.B., M.D., and Ph.D. degrees from the University of Minnesota. While interning in the Panama Canal Zone, he contracted tuberculosis. He spent one year at Glen Lake and Trudeau sanataria. After recovery, Wilmer became an instructor in pathology at the University of Minnesota, a National Research Council fellow in the medical sciences at Johns Hopkins Hospital, fellow in internal medicine and neuropsychiatry at the Mayo Clinic, and later a consultant in psychiatry at Mayo.

During the Korean War, he was in the Navy and retired as captain. His creative work in the Navy was the subject of an award-winning ABC docudrama, starring Lee Marvin with Arthur Kennedy as Wilmer. Bill Moyers produced two PBS-TV documentaries on Wilmer's work at the Salado institute.

Wilmer is married to Jane Harris. They raised five children.